OLD BLOOD FOR NEW SACRAMENTS

The Collected Poems of

Matt Borkowski

Iniquity Press/Vendetta Books

for my daughters Eugenia & Mary Elizabeth

Matthew John Borkowski August 4, 1951-April 15, 2017

some of these poems have been published in the following
books & magazines: Arbella, Ball Peen, Bee Hive, Big Hammer, Conceptual
Vandalism, Fierce Invalids: A Tribute to Arthur Rimbaud (Blind Dog Press),
Guillotine Broadside, Half Dozen of the Other, The Lion's Eye, Long Shot,
Lummox, New Jersey Bowel & Bladder Control, Street Value, Uptown Down!
(Iniquity Press,1999), The Reincarnation of Shelley and Other Poems (Iniquity
Press, 2017).

Joe Weil's introduction reprinted from Uptown Down!
Dwyer Jones' forward reprinted from _Home Planet News_

Iniquity Press/Vendetta Books are edited by Dave Roskos
Special Thanks to Angela Mark for her invaluable technical assistance

P.O. Box 906 Island Heights NJ 08736-0906
iniquitypress@hotmail.com

Front cover art by Matt Borkowski
Back cover photograph by Miriam Halliday-Borkowski
Cover design by Angela Mark

"Special thanks to James Wolffolk, American painter, 1947-1994, who
suggested the title Uptown-Down!. I was going to call it A Pillar of Salt, or
something else, equally ridiculous." --Matt

Special thanks Mary Fitzpatrick

Contents

Matt is neither a leftist nor a reactionary, neither a street poet nor an academic. He is a great American Crank, in the best tradition of W.C. Fields, Groucho Marx, Charles Ives, Hubert Selby, Algren...someone truly outside the establishment, including the anti-establishment.

Matt Borkowski cannot be read in comfort by either the right or the left. He is an ontologist of the dispossessed, the fucked up and broken beyond all class distinctions and political lines.

Borkowski spares no one in the realm of lifestyle leftism, including poets. He is down right brutal. It is the sort of brutality that preys not on the innocent and oppressed, but on the pretentious. We get "Ralph," the dentist poet who makes people listen to William Carlos Williams before he works on their teeth. We get the reincarnation of Shelley as a surly gas station attendant. We are told the "worst people in the world become poets." Somehow, we know it is true.

Matt doesn't even spare himself. His poems on his own impotence and sense of failure are forthright in a manner that offers a much needed alternative to the "I love myself" school of poetics.

Borkowski is not a positive thinker. He reminds us that love and integrity are difficult if not impossible, that the world does not easily conform to our expectations.

His mission is prophetic to the extent that he is letting us know we have all fallen short of the kingdom. He claims that "only people with no luck/really know luck/only those behind the fence know the distance." Matt, as I've already said, is an ontologist, someone staked always to the ground zero of what it means to exist in a universe of incommensurates. Nothing gels, nothing goes untainted and yet he claims, "a walk is prayer if taken well." He is too good a poet to say whether the prayer is answered or not.

Perhaps the walking itself is the answer. To walk with "one foot in heaven/one in hell/upon the earth where all have fallen," is the poet's true job. Matt walks with his eyes wide open, and we receive the gift of that journey without having to suffer much of the damage it has cost him. In the end, Matt is vigilant for the rest of us, even when we'd prefer him to be less so. He has stayed awake to tell us that even God is cause for his concern: "I'm worried about God/the luck the poor don't have, the rotting breasts of light/glimpsed through the window."

Enough bullshit. This is a great book of poems, the best I've read in a long time. Enjoy it.

-- Joe Weil -- more or less 7/28/98

For those of us working in poetry in New Jersey, Matt Borkowski has been something of a local legend--and a rarity--the past few years. He doesn't read in public very often, is self-contained and private, and doesn't seek the spotlight as do various poets of lesser talent. But, as the saying goes, you have to pay attention to the quiet ones, because Borkowski's been busy all this time creating a powerful document of anger, regret, remorse, forgiveness, repulsion, mercy, and wounded compassion in the poems collected in this book.

There is an icy fury at the core of Borkowski's writing, a raw, Job-like indignation at what we should regretfully call the common indignities of American life that is unusual--too unusual--in current American literature. I would call it refreshing.

"What end of the whip are you on?" Borkowski asks in a poem of the same name. "For what end were you groomed and tuned and / trained?" In "Sunday at the Homeless Shelter," he turns his ire inward: "there are many geniuses here / with me in the homeless shelter, / and many more sleeping / under bridges / and on subway grates; / a genius is a person who / will not compromise their opinion. / we know we are right. / Amen."

There is tenderness, too: "there are such things as ghosts in alleys / and blazing stars that fail to shine. / there are such things: the frail and tragic-- / things of beauty, lost and lame." (When Angels Die).

And moral disgust, also: "most people don't believe the real / world has anything / to do / with itself anymore; / Lincoln's just the head on the penny, / hippopotamus dribble, / the old, old infamy, / another holiday. / spit and more spit / Most people don't care to / see the world / with its tongue stuck out, its eyes rolling, / its nose twitch twitching sneezing yellow / pus." (After Reading Spengler {in the toilet}).

"Golem" is the centerpiece of the book. Like the brutish, barely animate clay man of Hebrew lore, its main character is a post modern Babbitt. Like his antecedent in the 1920s Sinclair Lewis novel, he is self-congratulating, prosperous, materialist, always chasing some bleak entertainment or distraction to fill in the abundant white space in his life. This golem is a construct of his socio-economic environs, a petit bourgeois, voting Democratic but thinking Republican and talking libertarian--the bogeyman byproduct of our present prosperity. He is what used to be called a "get-along, go-along" guy, the kind that accepts all convention, no matter how Darwinian, no matter how moronic, and doesn't wonder why the government has built a concentration *lager* next door to his neighborhood, as long as his pockets and belly are full: "perusing the white lines, / he likes what he sees, the neat rowed boxes / stacked on pallets filled with severed heads / waiting for shipment should bring a good price, / yes. Golem adjusts his flag pin, / runs his thumbnail / down his / red vest, / Golem is pleased, he will tell Mrs. Golem tonight over dinner, / they may be able to afford / the summer home in the Hamptons, / after all."

The fact that this is a deeply moral work will make its passage more difficult with those readers--and there are all too many of them--that have lost or never learned the understanding of irony. It will also not reach those for whom morality means preaching, judgement, and condemnation. But those readers that admire the subtle turn of phrase, the quiet epiphany, or the fair-minded double conclusion that everyone is a sinner and everyone deserves forgiveness, will find satisfaction in reading this book.

This is also a mature work wrought out of hard-won experience that is observed in a deceptively laconic style, through the eyes of a long-term prisoner of life. Borkowski's work, however, is not afflicted with the standard lazy cynicism so common across all contemporary media; his is the voice of a disillusioned romantic picking his way through psychic ruins and blasted dreams. Essentially, he is a true-believer in life, which is what makes the inner torment revealed in these poems so poignant. Inevitably--like a little death--we all experience the shattering realization that life is not under our control, that despair is always stalking joy, and that we may have to work very hard to defend our existence. Even after a full life of effort there is no guarantee of victory, honor, or even recognition. If this is what is sometimes called grace, it is no picnic. But to a gifted writer like Borkowski, it makes for deeply affecting poetic material. The writer pays the price of catharsis and delivers realization to the audience.

It would be wrong to leave the impression that Borkowski's work is drearily preoccupied with suffering, because it is not. Actually, often it's quite funny, although the humor tends to be sardonic and arch rather than obvious. But when it scores, it hits the mark solidly. There is "The King of King of Kings," which is truly one of the funniest pieces of writing--poetry or prose--that I've read in a long time. In the poem, we find ourselves standing before a display counter in a five-and-dime store arrayed with various mass-produced icons of the American mythos, heroes reduced to effigies manufactured in other countries by convicts or no-minimum-wage piece workers: "John Wayne is there. And Jesus Christ. Elvis Presley. / But where was J.F.K.? They always used to have him there. / Well, I guess he doesn't sell anymore. They only have / so much room. In a few weeks they'll probably have / the seven astronauts that died aboard the *Challenger*, they're / probably on order now, just waiting to come in. Anyway, / these are our heroes, our divinities....nothing enhances / life as death...the greatest heroes of our culture, / just two aisles down from the goldfish bowls...for 16 dollars and 98 cents you can hang them proudly...in your/ rec-room...or your basement...above your sofa or over / your bed...smoke a couple joints an' wham!....they seem to move...an' they're all yours, folks.... / Is our society this sick?! Yeah, you bet! // Black velvet paintings. An international commodity more stable / than any currency...These are our Gods, / ...the greatest heroes of our culture brought down to the / lowest common denominator.......William Carlos Williams / said, "the pure products of America go crazy." ....and he wasn't joking."

Nor is Matt Borkowski, to our greater benefit.

-- Dwyer Jones

A Walk Is A Prayer

a walk is a prayer if taken well,
one foot in heaven,
one in hell;

upon the earth where all have fallen,
a walk is a prayer

The Father In The Hallow Moon

the father in the hallow moon
swooning sins upon the harp,
in monocles and follicles
he weaves the web that guides the heart.

rather a demon glazed in frost,
with fast foot thunder on the run,
than patient logic, neatly coursed,
to lead a life that's never won.

the father's arm is wisdom's aim,
it rests upon a throne,
and when it rises through the air
the gutter calls the vagrant home.

When Angels Die

time and it's headstone misplaced on a mantle,
destroying even the taste of words;
these are the things that form the tomb.

these are the things: their monuments rotted;
asking not even their fallen king,
for one last silent sigh.

there are such things as ghosts in alleys
and blazing stars that fail to shine.
there are such things: the frail and tragic--
things of beauty, lost and lame.

Over moons and cracked windows, the mongrel sun
hangs dumb; and silence seeks shelter beneath its shade,

destroying even fleshy ghosts within its web of flame

These are the things! (all poets cry)
For silence sings when angels die

Poor Van Gogh

Poor Van Gogh
    your tortured soul
    lies melted now
           dissolved in stars,

    your burden reeks
      yet stands unbound

         as weeds of wisdom
      pierce the ground.

so little we know

    (being children of stone)

of how our forepast fathers fell--

    alone
        in fear no words can tell,

      so still in their silence
          our sorrows dwell.

Time is the father
    that quells our pain

    but yet in dust

      our tears remain

(strange how gusts of sunlit breeze

    can strip the frost from morning leaves)

Luck

God is luck to the luckless,
God is a bartender in the Bronx without any teeth

only people w/ no luck
really know luck,

only those behind the fence
know the distance,

only people who hate God need Him or Her or It.

God is the Ace of Spades,
just before it
slams you.

I'm worried about God,

the luck the poor don't have,

the rotting breasts of light
glimpsed through the
window

Like a Naked River

there never was a snake in all of Eden,

zebras, yes
            thousands of em',
          multi-colored ones,
peacocks too,
                (at least a dozen)
          but snakes,
                        no.

Adam was rolling in the grass
grabbing Eve all over the place--
          she told him where to shove it!

a zebra strolled casually by,
confronting a peacock near a small brook.

there never was a snake at all.

the apple myth is simply false,
a misunderstanding by the stream

they couldn't understand each other's colors,
became confused

began writing poetry
and eventually turned themselves into rainbows.

the snake came later
seeking the pot of gold,

and talking sex
like a naked
river

THE REINCARNATION OF SHELLEY

the reincarnation of Shelley pumps gas on
    the corner of Commercial and Handy,

    blows his credibility at the foodstamp office,

    tries to cut his wrist in a public toilet,
    fails; and calls collect Miami--an old girlfriend
    won't accept the charges

    "I'm too good," he thinks to himself, "too good
    for my own good, that's what's gonna kill me."
    etc., and next life I'll probably come back as a
    backgammon set, near someone's swimming pool, and then
    they'll appreciate me, I bet...................

the reincarnation of Shelley says weird things, like--
    "a cigarette...one cigarette...can keep you from
    losing your mind"...
    jailhouse talk, ya know? ...and
the reincarnation of Shelley has never even been to jail,

    but he's pissed...he relates to Black men
    in cages,
    has read LeRoi Jones,
    thinks Hinkley should be canonized,

the reincarnation of Shelley is a sick dude,
    but he knows it,
    wears a cross now, too,
    no more atheist shit,

    oh no,

    but he isn't mellow either,
    bet your ass he's angry,

"regular or unleaded," ...he hisses, when
you drive in,

"and pull up a little,
I can't reach the tank..."

GUILLOTINE

I carved initials in stained glass
    they ran like blood in flame
your arm
       an act of avarice
   a joke upon the plate

they stunk like burning rubber
    I saw each street a gutter
    and prayed to saints in agony
       to have my eyes removed

    your parasol through windows crawl
to hunchbacked children
           stuck in stalls
   to which all the rejected call
    to spit upon your gate

WHAT END OF THE WHIP ARE YOU ON?

what end of THE WHIP are you on?
in the collective morality
con.
lash centrifugal,
handle home,
sun drenched pavements
contribute

nothing.

what end of THE WHIP are you on?
security junkie faun?
baby blue metal charioteer?

what end of THE WHIP are you on?
        (the handle doesn't feel the heat,
    the weight
          of the
          LASH,
             the
        GASH   IT
            RIPS   the
      backs of
          tear-soaked concubines, who sew
    your bloody   shoes.
what end of THE WHIP are you on?
in the HUGE MORALITY CON!!!!
for what end were you groomed and tuned and
trained?

the handle world's a home,
the RIP of the LASH,
its
  GASH,
    only the
OUTSIDE
    knows;
what end of THE WHIP are you on?

Pride

Pride stroked the long of
the serpent's plumes,

the concrete maze of business sense,

broke the bells and broke the children,
broke the leaning of the fence;

Pride cracked the dry bone,
the furied sea,
the ram's horn,
the dumb sound,
the bird's wing,
the fish fin,
the lute string;

Pride buried half the world,
and the other half
we don't know,

Ah, the sting of moon glow!

20th Century Virtue

20th Cenury Virtue equals: Abandon
repeat:
20th Century Virtue equals: Abandon

sick to our gills we call to the
drunken captain of this ship,
like some Vandal soldier tired of
plunder and rape;

20th Century Virtue equals: Abandon

how many Blake scholars yawn
                and roll over coffee and cake
aching from discussion?   while the head of the
Department examines their wives cleavage, knowing all
too well

20th Century Virtue equals: Abandon

robbing a gas station with a stick,
"God told me to do it," he tells the judge,
knowing the goons are always hungry
and all have HBO

Penelope says the question answers itself,
            it cost her 400 bucks for the retreat
hell, I coulda told her, and for the price of
a beer,

20th Century Virtue equals: Abandon

How many deaths? How many abortions do we need? How
many Christs do we have to nail to the wall,
before we believe in simple mercy?

              (if I could play your voice upon
        a thread,
                  the spindle'd   CRACK,   and
        yet,.......)
        I've   heard them   sing.
        I've   heard them   laugh,
but still,   their laughter only proves...........

that Apeneck Sweeney smelled the crotch of dogs
that sat upon his knees
(but Sweeney fast repented)
and we all know that Sweeney hides
behind a dress,
a dress so old, its fabric like a shroud;

we all know Sweeney's dogs,...

they bid us for our jobs;

they lie on rugs of vertigo,
not even Oriental,
(beneath the smell of Sweeney's bones)

we all know Sweeney's bones;
"relax and enjoy life," she said, not
wishing to cause a fight,
"my nerves are very bad tonight."

and we all know Sweeney's smell,......

and surely,

if a smell   could walk

and talk,
        (how like a man?)
and rise upon it's
feet

        (once more)
and climb the stairs
it used to   haunt,

the smell would surely
say:

20th Century Virtue equals: Abandon

The Moon Withdraws From Human Sight

The moon withdraws from human sight,
            a sorry cloud perhaps has moved
        and bled across the night.

a young girl moans between her sheets,
the watchman hisses in his sleep,
        the moon is almost left alone,....

tide is guilty in it's roar,
                    it pounds like fever's blood,
moon is faultless in it's quiet
ageless in its hidden heat.

the watchman wakes and views the scene,
    his eyes like wrinkles   see no light,

yet tide and moon are one tonight
together on the shore

QUETZALCOATL $%#&*+!! ??

(a draft)

(pronounced ket-zel-ko-ottle)

I tire of picking dead sparrows
off the pavements at Easter,
Lord Quetzalcoatl, when are
you coming back?

     robes of purple and
heads on platters,

never heard of Cortez?--- you're lucky!

     ceilings   taped with stars,
chains hung from wrists
of   HOLY ABANDON,
seeking pity for the human race (a noble task)
Standard Dragon Repair Manual, an absolute
necessity
and

moons taped to
windows.

       Oh Doubtful
ROSE!
     and the daggered flowers
Lord Quetzalcoatl-----
       lift them
          up!

smell of fresh blood
     and
       bullet
         showers,

Lord Quetzalcoatl---

        lift them
         up!

     catch the
thorns of

      PARADISE,

       SHAKE EM'

BARE!

DOG

between the sun and
the ass sweat
dog (DOG)

PICKS UP the scent of fear.

(nobodies fault but your own)

in your own   country

    between the sun and
the ass sweat
dog (DOG)

taught you the rules.

because you suck the shoes of power,
you obeyed.
because your God is greed and tinsel and lust,
you obeyed.
    (when the
immovable force of centuries meet
centuries)

dog (DOG)
RULES.

Inside the chambers you decry, ignore;

rules the tramp of overturned
trash cans,....

the old gourmet,...
DOG.--
grinder of bones, and cute,... a good pal,
layered in incinerators.

of the indomitable spirit meeting the indomitable
spirit,...or at least,...at best,...
        a gunshot wound,........

Ashtoreth

why piss in the sink?--when
Ashtoreth is holding her Oriental
robin,

as a rose caresses the floor.

Is nothing sacred in this dream we
call our burden?

    -a bouquet of telephones
        wire the latest crucifixion on a
dare,
    her face,
        her vase,
   so pale,
       no moon,
    three swans;

a faint outline next to the bureau.

she never moves, never winks,
  our urine is
rain   and
foolish

starts;

and vanity,
Vanity,

in her arms

the world a sad toy,

two spiders mate on the
crease of her gown,

another nation falls to
Ruin,

as you turn the faucet closed
again

After Reading Spengler (in the toilet)

old spring is hung round the necks of whales
paint the flabby underbellies,
long the thin manes of cancerous giraffe,
stones of Germanic philosophy;

give us a new equation!

most people are fast to oblige
most people don't believe the real
world has anything
to do
with itself anymore;

Lincoln's just the head on the penny,

hippopotamus dribble,
the old, old infamy,   another holiday.

spit and more spit
                    Most people don't care to
see the world   with it's tongue stuck   out,
          it's eyes rolling,
   it's nose twitch twitching sneezing   yellow
pus.

          PROXIMITY,   is everything

     face the facts.
shred the Christmas new year with
the axe of the decimal, spark the tree limb once again.

HISTORY IS SOUL IN PROGRESS, the weight of chains
on dead martyrs, whose names we can't even recall,

Balloon men all, spiked with vomit drums, they beat,
BEAT BEAT   old blood for new sacraments

for the hunger strikers

there's a stranger death than suicide,
where shoreline touches sand;
and dogs swim forests
circumventing
stars in martyrs' hands.

struck in silver like the chalice,
blood upon the altar flows;
harlots wash their veils in scarlet,
mermaids braids are hangman's ropes,...

in Londonderry and Belfast
mermaids braids are hangman's ropes!

there's a stranger death than innocence,
struck by the scales of justice blind,
trails of sorrows,
seasoned armies,
sacred empty tombs.....

The Shifting Balance of the Wheel

the shifting balance of the wheel
leans like a leaf,
it's poles reveal
a staggering Giant
shadow form
that guards the solemn
hangman's horn.

the twisting, turning of this leaf
veils heaven and all heaven's grief:
a sorrow which so strong could clasp
and break our souls as they were glass;

the deadly shaking of the rope
shook as a world abandoned Hope,
and let the milling crowds move by
for fear that they would
see his eyes--

which glowed a vengeance
God's alone,
if only for a moment,
then,
a terror seized his puppet hands
and he was just a man again

Late

the world was created in fifteen minutes,
the same time it will
take for the bus I am
waiting for to
arrive.

yes, fifteen minutes.

a unicorn with broken teeth
told me this dreadful truth
one time near a
lilly pad as
I sat detoxing
from despair.

The bus I am waiting for took longer to make.
It was made by
greasy men with
greasy hands most of whom
hated their jobs, but did it anyway
cause they like
to eat.

they did not know me,
and they did not know
someday i would be
waiting for something they made;

it's always that way.

Their effect on my life has been
monumental;

Their bus is an instrument
of exquisite torture,
and it
may be late.

Ever since the world was first
created (in fifteen minutes)
lateness has been a
constant factor in
man's development.

Lateness has contributed to
more misery than possibly
any aspect of
our existence, other
than maybe Greed and
Fear.

when terrible things happen they
are always on time;

but when things
are late,

well,
we can only
wonder,

and wait

A Certain Wisdom

I watched her ass move
down the street, and I thought
to myself,
there's a certain wisdom to the way she moves

that'll make a man work all week long.

Hispanic,
19,
black patent leather pants, tight
red blouse,
white heels 6 inches high;

with short Pat Benatar hair, and
eyes and lips pouting.

I watched 3 dudes walk up to her,
and follow her along
down the street.

She's the prize
in a world
they'll never get out of.

19,
firm tits,
in her tight black pants
and white
stiletto heels,

yeah, that's somethin' a man'll work all week for;
an' to have a son he can name Miguel, after his grandpa,
an' have a blue Pontiac convertible
with fuzzy dice hangin'
from the mirror.

An' I watched her move
on down the street, with
her 3 suitors,
these Hispanic dudes,

an' I thought how these three guys probably all work
together in some recycling plant in Fords or South Amboy,
where people bring old books and newspapers,
an' they grind em' into pulp,
an' make cardboard out of em', an' paper bags for the
super market,
an' I thought, ya know,

there's a certain wisdom in
that
too

****

the give and take
of this tumbling
conception,
hardly hiding a new face
ground to pulp,

says, chance is the law on the windy streets,.....

servants doubt the deep of sleep,
and time is a liar
on the creep,

and chance is the law
on the windy streets,........

Throop Avenue

she tells me I shouldn't say we "have sex"
she tells me
        I should say we "make love."
I'm not sure.

I grew up on Throop Avenue when I was 28 years old,
it was Thanksgiving Day;

I had a can of Chunky Turkey Soup in my furnished
room,...I didn't have a can opener (I couldn't afford one),
.....I didn't have a hot plate either.

I had no visitors and
the drunk in the next room didn't have a can opener,
so I sure as hell didn't invite him.

I opened the can of turkey soup by pounding
a knife into the top with a brick I found
outside on the sidewalk;
then I tried to turn on the tiny A.M. radio
the junky downstairs sold me for a dollar,
but the battery was dead.

So after I ate the cold turkey soup
I masterbated in silence.

ON THROOP AVENUE PEOPLE HAVE SEX.

I grew up on Throop Avenue when I was 28 years old.

Children love their mothers,...I've seen it,...
mothers love their children,...(sometimes too much),...
I've seen that, too...

but men and women?

They have sex, I think.

the covers of the women's magazines beam off the newsstands
down town, with articles like--<u>50 New Ways To Make Love</u>,
.....and <u>Is Your Lover's Love Making Still Exciting?</u>,.....etc.,

but they don't fool me,.....

THESE WOMEN HAVE SEX

I grew up on Throop Avenue, when I was 28 years old,
with a brick on the floor, my cock in one hand, and a
dead battery in the other,...but now she tells me I shouldn't
say we have sex,....I should say we
make love,...

O.K.,...I answer,...
let's make love,......
but after it's over,
will we still like each other?

French Street Lullaby

I couldn't sleep.

so I sat at the window on the second floor.
I couldn't see the street light, but
it blazed off the bumper
of a big Pontiac and
hit me in the eye.

a guy stood near the car, all dressed up like
he was goin' to some big wedding
somewhere;
an' a woman, too; in red and white,
but then I saw her grab the back of his neck
real fast and knock his head
into the trunk of
the Pontiac.   (pound)

a truck rolled by and blocked my view. But

then   I saw him jump
back, an'
I mean
BACK;

an' shake his jacket off, and scream--

WOMAN   WOMAN!   Don't EVER do that!

he continued to brush his jacket off, while the
woman circled round the car a couple times, an'

another truck rolled by.

when it passed, he had HER HEAD AND
HE WAS slammin' it on the Pontiac's fender
like it was a mallet, yellin'

BITCH BITCH!

then two long trucks passed   and
after they passed this man
and woman were huggin' PASSIONATELY an'

and then she moved back a little and

placed her hand on his shoulder,

an' another truck rolled by an'
I couldn't hear what they
were sayin'

so I figured it was a damn good
time to pull the
shade down

I Ate the Word

I ate the word Love and spat it out;
and the subway shook beneath my feet,
and it's walls of stone quaked.

I ate the word Joy, and spat it out, too;
and 10 thousand children
sat on my knees and
laughed in my eyes.

I ate the word Hate and the
sorrow it's caused,
and I cried until morning
and still wasn't cured….

Then I ate the word God,
and spat it out,
and 12 thousand feathers fell at my feet,
and a silence arose,...

and so I left all words behind,
as others have done
when meanings lose their form;

and the night took hold,
and I watched the sky
unveil my
murders

Rainbows of God's Vast Face Receding

rainbows of God's vast face receding,
leaving some fat King once again;

I tire watching Death's gentlemen slaughter
innocence,
              (so I order another beer,
and watch my time dissolve to foolishness,
...and worry about my daughter's education)

suicidal showers, though, even now,....
sometimes make the best love letters;

and that, being a lie;.....only proves I
have been dreaming.....

Then when the local talent hunters leave bitterly,
I react like some old rancid priest,
dishing out dead flowers to the numberless
prisoners of freedom;

and yes,...in the black and white of Chaucerian
sit-com piss,....I am only a blank domino,...
and those who hate me
always survive

Tear Flesh from Bone

tear flesh from bone,
and heart from soul;
oh wind,
      and soul from me;
  as if the eye could
ever see or
  weep our sorrows,
--no such sea!

tear hate from love
and love from hate,
  despair from hope--
Oh miseries!--
   and dreams from time;
our spun designs of
selves unwind.....

clasp puppet strings
which we call gods,
and circus rings
   of sunset fogs,
and horns of plenty
we decide to wear, or burn,
or set
aside

for Mary's hair

when a cloud breaks,
when a wave parts,
when a storm brews
over crests of sky;

when a dream aches,
when a sea roars,
when a gull dives
through the cold air;

when a child cries
in her mother's arms;
when the wheel turns
in the playground,

are her feelings hurt?
are her tears dry?

when a song smiles
in a hot sun,
when the sound laughs
like a big drum;

when it falls
on her shoulders,

are her plans done?

if what could be (and what is, met)

if <u>what</u> <u>could</u> <u>be</u>
and <u>what</u> <u>is</u>   met,
their speech would speak of
sad
regret;

and <u>what</u> <u>has</u> <u>been</u>
would take a seat,
and feel the onslaught of
their heat.

when laughs and longings,
aches and tears,
collect disarming our
short years,
then   <u>what</u> <u>of</u> <u>all</u> we
could have been,
would choke and shake our
patience thin;

and TIME that monarch,
vast and cruel, who sits
upon us as a ghoul,
would stick his teeth into
our shins, and chew awhile
to hide his grin

GOLEM

clay wedding figure
straddles yellow line
three ton flame follows
Golem home

seeking some vanishing point
the crack under the door shouldn't admit light
but it does,

news from the bureau hasn't been good,

but Golem denies it,

the company needs a new trademark, can't move
enough people with the old one;

so Golem sends 40 tons of bananas overseas to
Compensate,
and curses the gamble, but what can he do?
it's sink or swim,
damns the old emblem, it's silly colors

Golem Tuesday Morning

Golem brushes his teeth, shines his shoes
factories out like a thick law journal praising progress,
every creed wilts celebration under Golem,

who makes dog food out of their hands and feet
sending helium balloons to the survivors

Golem Wednesday 2:17 P.M.

Golem goes to the dentist, mumbling "forgiveness is formlessness"
his dentist agrees, and tells him to dig the Tchaikovsky tape in
the elevator,
newsboy in wheelchair stares at Golem as he leaves

Golem feels compassion, not pity,
they should build more ramps, he thinks,
that's the way to go.

Golem Friday in the Warehouse

perusing the white lines,
he likes what he sees, the neat rowed boxes
stacked on pallets filled with severed heads
waiting for shipment should bring a good price,
yes.

Golem adjusts his flag pin,
runs his thumbnail
down his
red vest,

Golem is pleased, he will tell Mrs. Golem tonight over dinner,
they may be able to afford
the summer home in the Hamptons,
after all,

Golem turns aside,
away from the WORLD,

touches the soft aching flesh of his
prick through the hole in his pocket.

Monday is Golem's birthday, he's accomplished
much in his 43 years,

more than most
Golems,
and he never stumbled,
never faltered,

and most important,

this Golem ALWAYS KEPT IT CLEAN,

what the personal cost and aggravation....
and it hasn't been easy.

CLEAN GOLEM.

that's the miracle

Golem at Work, Golem at Play

Golem at a softball game,
Golem and more Golem.

Golem in the mountains,
Golem fishing in the sea,
Golem at a party,
Golem drinking tea,
Golem with new shoes,
Golem in sweat pants,
Golem naked
his right foot in the air,
Golem in the barber's chair.

Golem this and Golem that,
Golem.

Golem addressing a group of younger, yet rising
Golems,
Golem on a train platform,
the New York Times folded neatly under his arm,

Golem, in a lawn chair
sipping an ice cold beer,

Golem driving Mrs. Golem to her Aerobics class.

Golem alone.

Golem with Golem junior.

Golem drunk on New Year's Eve singing
"should old acquaintance be forgot!"
Golem sick on New Year's Day.
Golem yelling through the football game,
"Come on, COME ON!," pounding his fists
on the table,
Golem excited.

the many, many moods of Golem.

Golem visiting his dying father in the hospital
saying, "don't worry, you'll be O.K."
Golem lying.
Golem thinking, well, it's not the end of the world.
even the end of the world isn't the end of the world
to Golem.

Golem in despair,
Golem feigning charity.

Golem angry at the traffic
Golem, on the telephone complaining about
prices,

Golem greeting other Golems at a small gathering,
Golems everywhere.

Golem likes himself and other Golems,
or at least he tries to, that's the kind of
Golem he is.

kind Golem,
patient Golem,

and most important,
CLEAN GOLEM

Golem voting for his favorite candidate on November 5th,
Golem happy when his candidate wins,
Golem not surprised,
Golem says the tide has turned,
Golem knows things will get much better now.

Golem believes his country is the GREATEST COUNTRY IN
THE WHOLE WORLD!!!!!
Golem believes in freedom,
Golem sorry other Golems in other countries aren't
free like him,

Golem loves his freedom.

Freedom to be the kind of Golem he wants to be,
freedom to watch any show he wants on television,
freedom to read anything his Golem heart desires,
freedom to buy any kind of car he wants and finance it
through any bank he wants, with any type of payment plan
he wants,

freedom to drink any brand of soft drink he chooses,
anytime he chooses,
freedom not to drink soft drinks, freedom to say
fuck soft drinks, fuck all soft drinks,
I'll just drink water, Thank You.....

Golem thinks we should free the entire globe,
even if we have to use force,
even if we have to kill a lot of people in the
process.....they'll thank us for it
eventually,

Yes,
Golem and Mrs. Golem agree,

it's damn nice
being free

Why Poets Commit Suicide

the worst people in the world,
become poets,
Why?

to wring the worm in their soul?

Probably,
anyway I'd rather hear a banjo anytime

I'm selfish .

I wanna put God in a drawer,
away from everybody,
like
a gold
watch.

Why do poets commit suicide?
Why does anybody commit suicide?

cause they can't take it anymore,
that's why.

can't take what?

themselves.

the worst people become poets,

crying for an audience,
want to be loved,
all that.

it's not worth it,
wanting to be loved,

it never works.

any ass on the corner will tell you--

that's why poets commit suicide

THE COLD ROCK RIVER
of broken glass
     starts dark struck wind
     becoming stronger

    On State Street
    Dostoevsky kicks old ladies

    mules die too

    and after six the town folds
all but for the river
          and fat cops
     who eye holy whores
         and hair cream
    Lolita smiles
      to think back now
    how she knew Nietzsche
    in an alley

SUNDAY AT THE HOMELESS SHELTER

If Christ came back
we'd kill him again
this morning
 but he won't, so we can't.

and the staff is asleep,
and there's a child somewhere,
but not here;

here is failure personified on
40 bunk beds,
clothing from the Goodwill Mission
stuffed in crates underneath and
then some hanging limply drying
from the steam pipes.

there are many geniuses
here with me in the homeless shelter,
and many more sleeping
under bridges
and on subway grates;

a genius is a person who
will not compromise their opinion.

we know we are right.
Amen.

at night when all us geniuses
are sleeping, the fumes of
our thoughts climb towers
to our dreams,
and although our bodies are buried
in exhaust and humiliation,
we know we are right,
and time is a liar.

time is just a fat roach
to be crushed at tomorrow's
breakfast table, if we can
find one;
time is just a sweet little
blackhead on our noble cheeks,
to be squeezed and wiped
when the spirit moves us.

time is a liar.

we're not afraid of time; killing time is as easy as taking
a piss, an' cheaper, too;
the other geniuses and I know
the essence of time,
we know how to split a match
in half, and how to brush
our teeth with salt,
and how to make a dollar
last a whole day and then some....

an' how to roll a cigarette with one hand,
an' when to fight and when
to speak,
and when not to fight and when
not to speak,
and when to flush the toilet,
an' when not to flush the toilet,

the other geniuses and I are
DANGEROUS! --

no folks,
Einstein was not a genius.

he was just a fat little kid
with crazy hair--who excelled at something he
didn't really understand,

he'd never survive down here.

we'd squash him like a beetle
and watch his guts ooze out
his asshole--

no more gardens in Princeton,
no more atom bombs either;

we'd steal his tomatoes and
smash them in the street;
so much for relativity!

cause we know we are right,
and time....
well,

what time is it in Nagasaki?
don't know huh?

don't care either?

time is a cat with its eyes gouged out,
a bottle of cheap wine sucked down through
the phlegm of another day's
mercy killings;

we could care less if the whole damn machine
blew up right now, spitting blood and smoke
through these halls of hell,

we'd laugh,
bum another cigarette, an' maybe then,
wash out our socks and hang 'em
on the heat pipes,
for tomorrow.

so much for tomorrow

tomorrow--should it come--
will find us as we are
today--

content in our anger,

and not quite dead
enough
to
rise

TOMPKINS SQUARE

I

Sylvia's got a peace sign on her ass,
as I pick up cans to buy some tobacco;

the peace sign,--will it work?
nah,...not a chance,....

"Shake that thang!" shouts Ralph,
as she walks away, then she turns
round indignant, and gives him a
fuck you sign

II

puddles and puddles
of burnt-out faces,
and burnt-out brains;
as the midnight dragons stand on edges
and the lamp posts dance in flames

communist communicants steal
each other's duffle bags and books
to sell upon the street for drugs;...

the drugs?.....
and the puddles and puddles of
burnt-out brains

as the faggot cops patrol the paths
in their go-carts earning
32,000 a year

III

Friday's Hari Krishna night,
they come and bring us beans
and rice;
they don't throw God at us (they're alright),
unlike Sister Diana, who had soup
thrown in her face a couple weeks
ago, and now says things like,..."Where's
your friend,...he's an asshole,"...........or
"If ya didn't go to Bible study, then you can't
eat tonight,"....

who can blame her?
sometimes charity isn't
enough

IV

shades of Calcutta
in the dark American
death machine--

Bodhisattvas sleep in doorways,
under bridges and on subway grates,.....
WHY?
CAUSE THEY'RE LAZY, that's why,....
they DON'T WANNA WORK!!!

(but there is no work in the dark American
death machine night)

only piss in doorways,
and fake dollar bills
which litter the streets
in the yuppie stock market
video
kingdom

THE KING OF KINGS OF KINGS

Sometimes when I feel low I go to C.H. Martin's,
the five and ten dollar store on George Street.
It cheers me up somehow to browse....I check out the cancerous
parakeets.....look at mousetraps and jigsaw puzzles.....
and of course, who could resist their infamous black
velvet painting department?

All the really greats are there. It seems that one of
the highest honors our society can bestow upon a person after
they're dead is to sell their image on cheap black velvet
surrounded by a gaudy gold colored frame.

John Wayne is there. And Jesus Christ. Elvis Presley.
But where was J.F.K.? They always used to have him there.
Well, I guess he doesn't sell anymore. They only have
so much room. In a few weeks they'll probably have
the seven astronauts that died aboard the challenger, they're
probably on order on now, just waiting to come in. Anyway,
these are our heroes, our divinities....nothing enhances
life as death....the greatest heroes of our culture,
just two aisles down from the goldfish bowls....for 16
dollars and 98 cents you can hang em proudly....in your
rec-room....or your basement....above your sofa or over
your bed.....smoke a couple joints an' wham!.....they
seem to move....an' they're all yours, folks.....
Is our society this sick? Yeah, you bet!

Black velvet paintings. An international commodity more stable
than any currency....These are our Gods,
....the greatest heroes of our culture brought down to the
lowest common denominator....William Carlos Williams
said, "the pure products of America go crazy." ......and he
wasn't joking.

But Elvis didn't look like Elvis.....he looked more
like Ricky Ricardo....with sideburns....they must have
some lousy painters in Taiwan....they ought to pay them

better. And Jesus....well, who knows what he looked like?
John Wayne looked like John Wayne though....circa True Grit....
.....nineteen sixties. My mind fell into reverie.

Why didn't they ever make a movie with all these guys
together? It would have been a blockbuster! Business
isn't stupid......Hey.....wait a minute.....I was on to
something..... Yeah.....Maybe it's not too late.....so what
if they are dead?....they're more popular now than they were
alive. Death is nothing.....with enough financial backing
anything's possible.....This is America!

Sure, Elvis Presley in a musical version of the Christ story.
It can't miss. The ultimate Jesus movie. Starring Elvis
Presley....come back from the dead for one last movie.
The King himself....as the King of Kings....they could
call it THE KING OF KING OF KINGS! With an all-star,
all-dead cast in living color.....everyone's dead but the
audience. THE KING OF KING OF KINGS!

I can see it now:
The Greatest Movie ever made of the Greatest Story Ever
Told. The possibilities are endless. Fuck Death.....
the American Dream is bigger than Death.....it knows no
boundaries....no taste....only profit.....

The King of King of Kings! With an all-star all-dead
cast of thousands.
THINK OF IT! THINK OF THE PROMOTIONS,
THE ADVERTISEMENTS ALONE!

Elvis as Jesus. IF YOU LIKED THEM ALIVE,
YOU'LL LOVE 'EM DEAD! All direct from that vast
velvet painting in the sky! One last time.....the most
incredible encore in history.

with	James Dean	as John the Baptist
	Sal Mineo	as the Doubting Thomas
	Judy Garland	as the Holy Mother
	Marilyn Monroe	as Mary Magdalene
	Lenny Bruce	as Judas Iscariot
	Buddy Holly	as Saint Peter
	Richard Burton	as Pontius Pilate
	John Wayne	as the entire Roman army
	Vivian Leigh	as the woman at the well
	John Lennon	as John Lennon

(Hey, too bad Bob Dylan's still alive, he would've been great in this)

All direct from the grave for one last entertainment knockout!

SEE ELVIS-JESUS cure Rock Hudson of AIDS!

HEAR ELVIS-JESUS SING the Sermon on the Mount to 20 Thousand screaming, gyrating, all-dead fans!

SEE ELVIS-JESUS DANCE THE LAST JAILHOUSE ROCK after his arrest in the garden!

SEE THE KING OF KING OF KINGS! Directed by Orson Welles Screenplay by Jack Kerouac and Sylvia Plath. Director of Photography: Diane Arbus

CRUCIFIXION SCENE FILMED IN 3-D
DIRECTED BY SAM PECKINPAH

Homage to Checker

Chubby Checker was a very talented performer, he made "the twist" a national dance craze. I feel he hasn't really gotten the credit and respect he deserves. He brought joy to a large number of people, and most importantly, "the twist" was a very healthy phenomenon, it got a lot of people dancing and practicing physical exercise.

There wasn't anything negative about "the twist." Mr. Checker never advocated the use of drugs and if he used them, he kept their use a secret. Unlike future heroes of the musical industry (such as the Beatles, the Stones, Bob Dylan, the Grateful Dead), who flaunted the use of illegal substances, whereby encouraging their fans and followers to "thumb their noses" at the laws of our land, promoting an attitude of rebellion and it's inherent destructiveness.

Mr. Checker was "clean-cut." His music was simply for fun, plain and simple. True, he did steal the idea for his stage name from Fats Domino; but all artists are influenced by one another, and steal or "borrow" a little here and there. It's common knowledge. There is no great shame attached to a little borrowing. O.K., maybe he wasn't that original,...so what? He and Mr. Domino accepted the fact that they were slightly overweight; and a little fat, or "chubbiness" in the case of Mr. Checker,...was O.K. too. Some people just can't help being fat, there's a genetic factor involved, sometimes they don't even overeat, they can't help it.

So in addition to creating an enjoyable dance, Mr. Checker also made it alright to be a little fat or "chubby." Overweight people all over the country were no longer filled with shame and self-hatred. Some of them even dreamed of becoming musical stars themselves, and tried to invent their own original dances from scratch!

When the popularity of "the twist" began to fade in the mid-sixties, many people in the music industry started to claim that Checker was through, a has-been. But Checker proved his detractors wrong, by creating another dance craze with the "limbo rock" which involved trying to bend over backwards under a broom stick placed between two chairs. The height of the broom would then descend as the music proceeded. It combined, in a sense, the concept of a competitive game within a dance format.

More wholesome fun, and interesting, too.

Come back Mr. Checker, we need you. Where are you now? There are dances yet to be done. Knock Anti-Christ Superstar off the charts!

After We Eat

after we eat,

Miriam wants to go to the
used book store to
buy some old
National Geographics, preferably ones
with African features.

she wants to cut them up, cut out the
pictures, pictures of starving
children, and tape them all
over the inside of the
refrigerator, to
scare visitors.

shock them.
make them see how lucky they are.

she scares me sometimes. starving children
in the ice box;
this time she's gone too
far. But I'll never be able to talk her out of
it.

she says she did it in Arkansas, and
it worked perfectly.

"People shouldn't be fat," she says,
"Western decadence."

I tell her yeah and all, but--

"Isn't fatness it's own punishment, ya know?
I mean, fat people are usually pretty unhappy being
fat,....and anyway, I mean, it would be different
if the food they stopped eating could be
channeled to the starving children,

but it doesn't work
that way."

"yeah, " she says, "but something has to
be done..."

on the way home from the used book
store,
I get hungry and stop
and get a
slice
of pizza

with
extra
cheese

EUNUCH #1217

said poor Jeremy
9 years old

in 1376 A.D.

being led to
minor surgery

"But Your Worship,

I don't care to sing
like an
Angel!"

kneesocks and wires (Allen Unleashed)

"It's a good life, if you don't weaken," my grandma used to say,
and she always kept a good table.

Allen Swenson digs hard hats on little girls in kneesocks, he works
for the local Legal Board. Friday he puts on his black eye patch and
he's gone. But his Rabbi keeps it between friends. "There's already
enough gossip," he says. "And blood is the only thing they understand."

Allen Swenson buys organically grown peanuts from the local Lebanese
grocer and says he doesn't feel guilty about a fuckin' thing, even the time
he tried to strangle his girlfriend with a violin string because she didn't feel like
making love. They put her on Haldol for a couple of months and now
she's working as a dental assistant and says she loves it. Things work out.

Allen's into electronics now. Heath Kits. His entire apartment's wired. He
did it himself. He's watching the Wimbledon tournaments on a set he
assembled himself. Soup to nuts. If any Puerto Ricans try to break in and
steal anything while he's dreaming of kneesocks a sound will go off "like
the fuckers never heard. They'll think it's fuckin' World War III!" He did it
himself. With a soldering, a "lot of nerve," and Easy-To-Read instructions.
Soup to nuts. "The fuckers'll think the fuckin' roof is blowin' off!" And his
girlfriend will be the first to tell you it's true too, cause one night Allen
was out bowling and she forgot her key and climbed in through the window.
"It sounded like the Third World War," she smiles, "I thought I was gonna
piss my pants, I thought I was gonna get a heart attack, I was so scared!"
Allen did it himself.

He was always clever with building things. He was always good with his hands.
Once when he was a child he made a palm tree with an erector set. Even his
sister who was barely even four years old and who had never seen a palm
tree, knew what it was. At least that's how he tells the story.

Allen Swenson digs all kinds of construction, even mobiles and kites--ever
since he was a kid in kneesocks. His girlfriend wants to get married
in May, but Allen worries it might interfere with his bowling.

He likes all different kinds of cheeses. Sometimes for fun he goes out
and buys four or five different kinds, all at once. He even lets his girlfriend
try them. "You should try the one with the sesame seeds," he smiles, spreading
a soft cheese on a cracker. "O.K.," she smiles. She trusts Allen. She knows he'd
never say "try the one with the sesame seeds" unless he tried it first himself.
He's good that way. "When I was on Haldol everything tasted like plastic," she
laughs. "Try the one with the fuckin' sesame seeds," says Allen, "I have to
go out for a while."

"Where?" she asks.
"There's a sale on kneesocks at Franklin's," he tells her.

But actually he goes to see the Rabbi.

"She wants to get married in May," he tells him.
"Blood is the only thing they understand," says the Rabbi.
"My bowling team thinks I should wait at least until August."
"They may be right," nods the Rabbi.
"Did I tell you I have the whole place wired?"
"It's probably for the best," says the Rabbi,
"How long did it take?"
"Just a couple of days."

The Rabbi smiles. He understands such things.

"Well, I have to be going," says Allen.

"God bless you," says the Rabbi.

Once outside the door Allen puts on his black eye patch. If they try
to break in and steal anything they'll be sorry, he thinks to himself.

Yes, it's a good life.

Joseph K. Meets Marcus Swelby

Doctor Swelby and his assistant Killy just wouldn't give up on me.

It all started when I checked the organ donor box on the back of my driver's license. I did it as a joke. I mean who in the hell would want my already cirrhotic liver and my failing heart of stone?

Well anyway, his receptionist Consweata called me the very next day and insisted I accept an invitation to the Doctor's house Friday evening for a surf and turf dinner with all the trimmings, to be followed by a free check up.

I hung up thinking it was my ex-wife calling from the mental hospital again, she does that sometimes when she has the money.

But to make a long story short, it really was Consweata. And Swelby and Killy came over the next day. Just by looking at me they knew I was going to die.

Of course they didn't come right out and say it. They just started hanging out all the time, taking my kids to the circus and baseball games. Killy started parking his motorcycle on my front lawn.

When I told him to get his fucking Harley Davidson off my goddamn lawn ....he just gave me a strange grin and said, "I don't know how to ride it.....I forgot."

Consweata kept bumping into my current wife, who isn't much saner than my ex-one, at the shopping malls and church functions, which was very strange since they're both atheists. They became great friends and started exchanging cake recipes and fashion tips.

The whole thing smelled rotten to me. I didn't like it. And I started getting scared. But the funny thing was that physically I had never felt better in my whole life. Really.

Then one day I just passed out on my front lawn.

Of course Swelby was there in two seconds in his beige sweater and golf shoes and carried me to the hospital on his back.

When I woke up everyone I knew was gathered around my bed. Even my ex-wife from the nut house, she said she forgave me for driving her insane; my kids were there......my now-wife....she said she forgave me for everything I ever did wrong and changed her mind and now believes in God.....Swelby insisted I just call him Mark.....and not get excited.....Killy just smiled and said he'd be moving his motorcycle from off my front lawn in a couple days.

"How long do I have?" I screamed. "I can't die, I don't have any medical coverage!"

"Don't worry about that now," said Swelby. "I'll pay for it out of my own pocket.....if necessary.....anyway, that's the least of your concerns right now.....just try to relax...."

"I don't wanna die!" I shouted.

My two wives and all the kids started crying.....Swelby put his arms around them and invited everybody over to his house for coffee and donuts......till it was over.

TILL IT WAS OVER.........IT WAS ME!

They all departed weeping. Consweata was taking my children to Great Adventure Park to go on the rides.....but the little one kept screaming, saying she would rather go to Chuck E. Cheese to play video games.

Everyone left but Killy.

"I don't wanna die! I don't wanna die!" I told him.

Then Killy stopped grinning and approached my bed.

"Look, stop feeling sorry for yourself," he said. He said it with such firm kindness I knew he must be right.

"You're right," I said. He sure made a lot of sense. And it was his stern, no nonsense attitude that convinced me. I guess I was feeling sorry for myself. I mean everybody dies, right?

"I'm sorry I was feeling sorry for myself," I said. "So what if I die, it's no big deal, right?"

"Now ya got it!"

He won me over....with his simple logic. What a guy....and ya know the next thing I knew I was dead....and it wasn't so bad...........

I just hope he moves that motorcycle.

Nice

What is nice? Sure, people always say have a nice day. Yeah, right. But what is it?

We say he's a nice person, or -- she -- she's nice. But what the hell is it?

Yeah, O.K.,...most people would agree that say Willard Scott, the T.V. weatherman, seems like a nice person. Agreed?

And he IS A NICE GUY. In fact, he's made an entire career out of being nice. He's too nice. I hate him. But that's besides the point, and enough about Willard, for now.

Let's get back to nice.

Nice is a nice word. And it's nice to be nice. It's nice to have a nice day.

But what is it?

It's a sunny day. A warm day. And you don't get a headache. And you don't get mugged. And your wife is nice to you, if you have one. It's nice to have a nice wife.

Nice.

The sun is nice.

God made the sun, so he must be nice, ... sometimes.

But what about rain and earthquakes and wives that cheat, and loneliness, poverty and disease?

They're not nice.

How could a nice God make mean things? --

How? Well, I guess the answer's simply, he didn't make them.

The Devil makes them.

Anything not nice is the Devil's business. He's not a nice guy, and we're not surprised that he isn't.

Willard Scott doesn't like him either. He causes too much trouble. Willard Scott almost met the Devil once on one of his many cross country crusades of niceness. He almost met the Devil and the Devil, being what he is, was not being nice. The Devil, in fact, created a series of tornadoes and hailstorms in the center of Kansas which were not nice at all, and Willard Scott had to leave in a hurry and take all the people he worked with with him; for they were out there to televise the celebration of Ruthie Mahoney's one hundred and fifth birthday, which would have been really nice had it occurred.

Willard had brought a huge cake and funny hats and streamers and horns and his whole entourage to the middle of Kansas, and Ruthie had been waiting for weeks for this incredible party to be televised on National television and she truly deserved it after having survived so long and having been sweet and kind and nice to almost everybody she had ever met in the course of her long life in an often not nice world.

Ruthie was ever so happy and excited anticipating the big party with Willard, who is more than likely one of the nicest people on television today when all of a sudden just 92 minutes before the event was scheduled to take place, the Devil (it must have been) created a fierce and sudden tornado with hail also which descended upon poor Ruthie's humble dwelling at 17 Delancey Street in a quick descent without any warning whatsoever, leveling the house to rubble and driving her deceased husband's five iron through her very forehead in two-thirds of a second, totally ruining any chance of her long anticipated meeting with Willard,

and that's not nice.

She didn't have a nice day at all!
As much as Willard would have liked it to have been nice, it simply wasn't.
Willard and his crew showed up 23 minutes later in the Network van. They had a very nice ride to Delancey Street, after having a terrific breakfast at the Hyatt Regency in Lawrence, Kansas, the food was excellent and the service couldn't be beat. On that they all agreed.
But when they drove up to where Ruthie's house used to be they did a double take, for between numbers 15 and 19 Delancey Street where Ruthie's number 17 had stood well fixed only 23 minutes before stood nothing but an old rusty pipe which had earlier been connected to a now non-existent washing machine. Nothing else. Not even a couple of old yellowed photographs. Nothing. Just a rusty pipe sticking up out of the ground. Her neighbors' homes were there intact, not even a scratch on them.
Willard stared in startled amazement. He tasted the lingering remains of the sausage and egg buffet at the Hyatt, courageously suppressing a burp.
He wondered where her house was.
Willard had just missed meeting the Devil.
Ruth Mahoney wasn't as lucky. Her entire day had been ruined.
She didn't have a nice day.
No, ... it wasn't nice at all.
What did Willard do? Well, ...what could he do? Obviously, the show was ruined. He realized that after a few minutes. Ruth Mahoney's neighbors stood outside their houses staring in disbelief at the rusty pipe and Willard's Network van. Mrs. Arnold, Ruthie's neighbor and closest friend testified through tear soaked eyes that Ruthie probably would not be returning for the rest of the day.
Her birthday celebration was indefinitely postponed.
Willard suppressed another burp, although this time with a little more difficulty, and then said to his crew as nicely as possible under the circumstances --

"Folks, we better get the hell out of here!"

He didn't like to use the word Hell, …it was a bad word. And Willard doesn't like bad words, and he tries to avoid using them. They come from a bad place, the Devil's place. They aren't nice. He immediately caught himself, and then added humbly-

"I mean,..HECK,…this is terrible!"

And indeed it was.

It was terrible.

Everyone agreed.

Driving back to Lawrence in the Network van everyone was silent for the longest time, not knowing really what to say and also out of respect for Ruthie who they never really got to know very well, when Willard suddenly said--

"I mean, …I feel sort of responsible, you know, …I mean being a weatherman and all…"

"Willard, hey…don't blame yourself…" said Frank, the cameraman and a hell of a nice guy himself, "It was the will of God…that's all…"

"No, …no," said Willard. "Don't say that! God would never do anything like that…never!…I just can't understand why things like this happen,…it's not right. It isn't."

"You're a real nice person Willard,…you know that? You feel so deeply,…you really like people don't you?"

"Yeah,…I do,…"

"I bet Ruthie was a real nice woman."

"I bet she was," said Willard.

"The party would have been so nice."

"You bet," said Willard.

"It's all so sad."

"Yeah,…it is."

"Hey,…let's not get so morbid,…ya know! Hey Willard,…hey…Ruthie was a hundred and five,..ya know? She wouldn't want us to get all morbid…she wouldn't. Hey, look…you look like you need some coffee,…let's stop up ahead, there's a place comin' up in about a mile……we'll stop for coffee,…it's a real nice place, if I remember…fresh baked cakes and pies,…baked right on the premises,…whataya say?….huh?…"

"Yeah,…well," said Willard, "fresh baked pies?…ah,…yeah,…that might be nice,… baked right on the premises?…are you sure?"

"Willard,…it was almost three years ago,…I was out here to cover the riots,…but yeah,…it was nice,…a real nice place,…great pies and cheese danish,..the cheese danish was fantastic,… I just hope it's still there….."

The Leap

your leap made everybody
look --
that great falling,
for a moment,
the "what is it for-edness"
crystallized

not a pretty sight a man
plunging towards pavement
18 stories below.

what was it?   Why?
a bad marriage?,
a lost job?,
poor service at the diner?
something small, the last straw?
        a favorite show taken off the telly?, or big?--
        a troubled son on drugs?--
        a sexual problem?,--
        alcoholism?--

a combination of the
above,
or maybe just a total
overwhelming saturation
with the uselessness
of it all--

all our strivings don't amount to much,
do they?
all our sufferings,
all our hopes;

your leap was a spit in the eye of God,
or worse, of no
God,.....

maybe just a frozen pigeon under
a bridge,

but whatever it was,--
we looked and
stared in awe and wonder,
and gasped--

you made us see

we're all sorta just one person,
it's scary,

and someone watching,
someone with real good
eyes,

thought he saw
a smile
on those lips,...in fact...
a smile not so crazed at all,

and somehow also a
triumph,...which was
Godlike in
it's falling

        down

Postponing the Inevitable

I already had half a load on when
I walked into the Crown Tavern for a
couple more.

there was some folksinger there, singin'
"Baby, Mama, don't make me sleep on the floor tonight!"

Ralph was there, the dentist poet, he reads
William Carlos Williams to his patients before he
pulls their teeth. He brags about his days back in
Haight-Ashbury, before he went to dental school.

I always enjoy seeing Ralph.

How's it going Ralph? I said.

good, good, I'm REALLY STONED!
REALLY STONED!

you don't look it, I said,
what's new? what have you been reading lately?

ah,...Paterson Book II, he says.

what else is new? I ask.

I got a girlfriend now, he says.

really? what's her name?

Barbara, he says,....she's a real estate broker,
but very literate, I met her at an Italian film festival,
she writes,....she's very into Wallace Stevens,
writes sort of like him,
very symbolic,

sort of a cross between
Stevens and Hilda Doolittle, you know,
H.D.

did you get in her pants yet? I ask.

Hey, Matt, don't ask me that, I mean,
I really like her, man.

so you got in her pants? huh?

Hey, man, you're drunk,...don't talk like that,...

I'm sorry, I said.

well, O.K.,.....he said....I mean, I really like her,
she writes a lot like Hilda Doolittle,
very imagist,....
we're going to Mexico in the spring
for two weeks, to write and drink
tequila,...REAL TEQUILA....
an' go see where Hart Crane lived his
last months,
there's a museum there now, ya know....

Well, I said,....that's good, Crane was
good, real good, a good poet, in the
end he knew,....

what did he know? asked Ralph.

well, he knew,....a,......that,...a,...homosexuality
is a cop-out,....

oh, said Ralph.

an' he knew, that a,....well,....heterosexuality
is a cop-out,....

oh, said Ralph,....but what isn't a cop-out?....

well,....I guess, just postponing the inevitable!.....

death? you mean?..........he asked.

NO, LIFE!....................lend me ten dollars.

but he talked about Barbara and Mexico and Hilda
Doolittle, and root canal work,.....and Ezra Pound
and Sappho, and how the snot and mucus moves through
tear ducts and pores, and lodges in pockets above
molars.....
for an hour,

maybe more..........
till I really started wishing I was dead.

but he finally lent me five dollars.

an' so LOOK, I said, I gotta go, I'm waiting for
a call at home,.....an', he said bye, an' I said
thanks, an' he said he'd send me a postcard from
Mexico, and I said O.K.,

an' that being that,
I staggered off
into the asphalt night
as happy as a
pig in
shit

from The Drunken Poet's Survival Manual

preface: (list of do's & don'ts)

1-Take the LSAT and score brilliantly; then say fuck it and get a job
   in a sweatshop packing foam rubber all day.

2-Never read Hemingway, Kerouac, or Charles Bukowski;
   (you probably have already, if that's the case, stop
   immediately). It's not too late. If you really need idols,
   read Jeffers, Genet, Dante and the Bible.

3-Don't ever, I repeat, EVER, drink at The White Horse Tavern
   in New York City. It's DEATH for drunken poets, and besides,
   most of the people there are very boring.

4-Never go to relatives weddings!!!   If you really have to, and can't
   get out of it, leave immediately after the ceremony, before you get
   drunk and get thrown out.

5-If (I should probably say when) you get arrested; don't say nuthin'
   to your fellow inmates for at least 48 hours. Sleep with one eye open and
   don't bum any cigarettes. Find out where the cliques are, and avoid them.

6-Realize that Henry Miller was the greatest American writer since Herman
   Melville (they even have the same initials). But DON'T for God's sake, go
   live in Paris.

7-Never send any of your stuff to the New American Poetry Review, and
   bad-mouth it everywhere you go.

8-If you get involved with a woman, MAKE SURE she's the kind
   that'll buy you a pack of cigarettes when you're broke.

9-Find out where Gregory Corso is living at any given time. But don't try to
   contact him. It's just important to KNOW. (hey, it's alright; he doesn't like
   Allen Ginsberg anymore, either).

10-Make sure your furnished room has a sink and a working radiator. (The sink so you can piss in it and also wash your socks in it. The radiator so you can dry your socks on it and also to heat up canned spaghetti.

11-KEEP WRITING!!! (Even though death, poverty and insanity are always at your doorstep. Remember--they are probably the three best friends you have!)

The Grip

"I'll do anything to beat that grip,..." he said,
"that feeling like a vise,...the hopelessness,...
the grip of it,....I hate it,....

I hate that feeling,...I'll get drunk,...do dope,...
start fights,...throw money around,...right and
left,...borrow money, right and left,...leave my
girlfriend,...kick the dog,...anything,...anything
to kill that feeling,...when the grip gets you..."

"Yeah," I said, "I know what you mean,...I hate
that feelin' too,..."

he's dead now...
I'm still alive,...

I don't know why,
I knew exactly what he was talkin' about,

exactly,.....
boy, I hate that
fuckin' feeling

Sex Change

it was so weird,
she was the supervisor
tellin' us all how
to do this stupid
market research phone
survey job;

an' I was the only one there old
enough to know she
wasn't really a woman.

Yes, (I thought)
technology
has emasculated
both
of
us.

why think of it!
(I thought of it)
a virile young poetry genius
like me,
being forced by circumstances
beyond my control
to take this crummy job,
and this stupid broad (who's not even
a broad) tellin'
someone like ME
how to SAY   WORDS!

she was pretty good
at it though

Handcuffs, Eyes (I's), and Rimbaud's Mother

it's easy to turn the other cheek when you're in
handcuffs,...you have nowhere to go; everything
becomes shit,
beautiful shit

embroidered manure.

the man in the multi-colored hat is drinking malt liquor,
his wife is dying of virtue, no scorpion, or TWINS--
WHATEVER,
the man in the multi-colored face has no club to
join,

IT'S RAINING SOMEWHERE.   THIS IS ALCATRAZ!

behind the mask
a jeweled ass cries.

the sad girl in the pink slip is practicing karate,
she has nowhere to go, no clock to wind

her mother is dying of virtue, taking medication

she's dreaming of a new car, guitar;
Rimbaud in silhouette, Promethean rainbowed;
his mother is shaking a spider from a long branch,

she is weeping, she understands,

it's a long haul & everything is SHIT,
multi-colored shit.

I could have said I (I AM SHAKING A SPIDER FROM A
LONG BRANCH, I HAVE NOWHERE TO GO, etc.)

but BLANK (_____) knows enough not to say I (eye),

so the EYE (I), becomes transformed,
into Shakespearean cripples of LESS THAN EVEN ONE DIMENSION--

they have no real existence other than their bodies,

i.e., THEIR SPEAKING VOICES, ...the I, (eye) is
abolished,
unseen,

non existent,....and HENCE? EVERYTHING BECOMES SHIT
BEAUTIFUL EYELESS NON-POETIC SHIT!

smell it, taste it, roll it up in a ball, smear it on
the walls…………………..

it is Christian, it is Moslem,
whatever,
beautiful, tasteless, shit, …..the EYE (I)

being realized in namelessness, which does not none the
less eliminate suffering or DEATH, but
merely the sense of loss,
which is
NEVER, ever,
LOST.

        It's easy to turn the other
cheek when you're sleeping,

particularly when you're sleeping in
handcuffs;

        It's harder to die.

        It's harder to die trying not to say the
        word I,

It's harder yet to believe in the
word I

after you're
dead,

especially if you die in handcuffs, i.e., HANDCUFFS, i.e., ETC.,

it's harder
still to make love to
someone
3000 miles away,

harder even when they're
near.

and so, blank answers blank, eyeless, mercifully,

everything is shit,

beautiful shit,

tough as nails,
totally
unpoetic

MY DEAR UTOPIAN

(outside your time)

If I could a lilac
bloom between our
fragile fingers,
and the streams, tear blood,
I would and could
stop some immortal
sob;

It is a wasp that
grasps the air to hang
and dangle, there---
some beauty in a spell,
we will bring down
to our unearthly presence.--
in minuet so fair,
it blasts the nakedness
of bones and
rises on an air.

Only three strong winds
are left that
rise upon a crooked beat
and fast the parted
left-behind.

Should we embrace & leave
them there, to skip, slip
skip---
and rhyme?
My dear, my dear
utopian,
we haven't a chance
in a pig stye
played upon a cheap Victrola
this our hope,
our dream!

for Baby Fae

they've undone you famous baby--
made you spit death in black headlines,
ringing bells of Quasimodian agony, not
even a face or name;

dear child!

from the tower, the tower
Which we broke down, to
the polished chrome of
Armageddon,
falls no softer, purer
step than yours

you rang their bells.
the ghouls they all showed up
on time; and withered now
you're gone,

so blameless,
how could they know your form
so quickly gone?

for the lost, the lost so gaining power butchered your
human heart's last beat
and spun a web so
microscopic tears
the size of
mountains
bloom.

between the honk of the car horns, fumes of gas,
you were born, child;
blazing as the night we gave
our pledges out too soon

and fast forgot.

sand and sand.
sand and sand.
you rang their bells;
the ghouls they all showed out in force.

the light upon your forehead was a diamond birthmark,
the scar across your chest a travesty to Hippocrates;
and the tin foil skirted river
Acheron runs
deep
through the frown of Babylon.

        all we can know
     are visions,
             shadows,
    stabs of pain,
      lopsided dreams
   we place   on

   stools
          and leave
   behind.

a wasp,
 a dagger for our eyes,
      and to   survive   we beg   the blasted
worm
a moment more.

a tiny baby her real heart cut out, replaced,
an experiment.
her life

her death,
an experiment.

the vase upon our shelf so cracked

it smears reflections on our walls, of lopsided
dolls with hearts cut out, who cry real tears
for newsmen ghouls,
who drool their copy day by day;
a dark medallion
framed.

her doctors drove their Porsches home
to mink coat wives who nursed their grief
with tax exempt martinis!

an experiment!

we gathered near your burial lawn,
listening to radios
our eyes dissecting the real life within,
the crushed baby form made six
weeks of virtually constant drugged
half-alive PAIN!
A BED OF PAIN!

they held you to their ears,
their hearts lying aloud to the world.

an experiment!

a spot of life, dismembered of the Sacred Fist!
kept alive/killed the modern way,
the slow, slow, agonized   WAY!

OH, BLESSED TECHNOLOGY -- SAVIOR of humankind!

we lie at your heels,

OH GREAT CHROME WORM!
OH BLOODY SERPENT GREAT CHROME WORM!
WE KISS YOUR NAKED FEET!

DANCE OUR LAST DANCE

for a moment's absolution,
your   ten-horned LAST HOPE!
spitting water.

YOUR SEVEN HEADED ROAD TO HELL!

the quality of any life not deserving even a second look,
WE LICK YOUR HEELS!

as if the kindness of death had no God-drawn
strings,
it's dignity denied.

****

what can I do?   write more lame poems?   their structure
and content always awkward, always imperfect;

renew my library card? clean my imaginary rifle?
curse a world that tramples such innocence?

> they've undone you famous baby--
> us, me, them, ourselves.

> Goodbye!
> I wish I never heard of you.
> their MERCY has me terrified!

> such a short life--yours.
> but it should have been even shorter,
> less painful.

> tears
> unlimited and unquenched
> as yours
> should
> never be,
> sweet girl.

> and though you're gone--
> THE BEAST PREVAILS

Mantua

for Patti Smith

I stared into the darkest woods
beneath the sky of Mantua
darker than unknown herself,
I met her there

No diamond stars, the air was black
and heavy wet with tears
with what has been and disappeared

and left me here

two wolves sat distant there on high
I heard their cries
beneath the sky of Mantua,
I felt their signals pierce like claws
into my ears,
               and die
a sudden shriek, unholy cry

so wet with tears
with what has been and disappeared,
just as oppressive as the sound

of love's departing tears.

Her face was hidden by the trees,
a red scarf dangled on a branch,
and tore its way across the wind
of mystic blood which flows within
and disappears so unabsorbed

I met her there

Her breath ran sacred through the maze,

and pressed against the bark
so moist and bitter
was her smile
and crazed

it slashed across my heart

and left a pawn, so dry of life
the wind has nothing left to sort,
or drag along the side

her scream raged wild
through the air of Mantua

Flag of no nation

This is a flag, the latest flag, no,
the original flag, before
the flood, before the
blood, before the blood began to flow,
before the guns went off...

the flag of Non, the poet's dream
there are no boundaries, no laws

the flag of non...or no nation
non spelt backwards is Non...Non

before the curse of Hammurabi
before the Persian Wars
before the Incas danced like stars
before the red, before the Redman's crucifixion,
non,
before the blue
before our dreams turned blue
before the slaves
before Betsy Ross had intercourse with
industrial drain pipes
screwing countless hungry immigrants
making them mean, feeding evil, hate and disillusion
to their children,
before the flood
the flag of no
before McDonald's reamed out Exxon and poisoned our souls
with food like dirt,
and plastic clowns which never frown
and don't have keys for toilets, in cities, where starving
black hispanic white asian hobos,
can't even shit like dogs
for free

the flag of non, or no
before technological hell gave heat and formulae no one understands,
hell spelt forwards is hell,...HELL

before Babylon cut out our speaking tongues, making us
sad mimes of our own fears, unable to say the word LOVE
and mean it, without fear,...ever...
before the surgeons hand carved scalpel of green anger...
before we stopped even trying, for to survive we have to lie a lot...
98% of the time a conservative estimate, before we
believe our own lies...before prisons...
before the locked doors of Saint Vandalism...an act of love...
before Cain...before the lips of Jezebel...inspired color...
before the dress of Baptism
before circumcision...before Toys R Us became us having fun costs
lots of money
before the American death machine trampled our lives and
minds, with fear, fear, fear...it caught like fire...starting where?
...the very air we breathe...and then the walls began to grow, with paper
decorations...flowers...killing pores which used to breathe...
before the need to be number "one" killed EVERYTHING!!

this is the flag of man's and woman's last attempt to reconcile
...words like God...and Holy Holy
the bed sheet of communion...copulation...last try for communication...
before we die...and all go QUEER...from loneliness...

the flag of the body...
the last real death we breathe each day
before we accepted the word IMPOSSIBLE
to breathe the dust of love's impossibility...over
and over, and over...
the oldest lost Lenore

non spells non...no nation...creating the need
for Angels...see them come...and dreams...of miracle salvation...
every second...every second

see them come...and make our beds...with
feathers of forgiveness...how they cry...
I've heard them weeping wailing for our twisted dreams
they come like armies in the clouds

Non spelt wrong is Non,...Non
a body of disheveled dirty malcontents...
angels...etc. patriots...
are now forming...they're all full of shit...and yet...but...
forming forming
forming against the backdrop of computerized Hell...
spelt Hell ...angels with bodies...bowel movements
sexual movements...
disheveled...yet gaining direction...seeking...
forming beyond institutional jargon...
beyond format...beyond the shitty "concept" flag...
beyond this lousy poem
no nation...absolutely none...that's right
...as soon as we find out where it's gonna be
its exact latitude and longitude will be announced
probably in the Targum...at least...
thanks for listening

KONGORIKISHI

grey stone serpent
                    flowered death
        the deep carved idol's eyes

is hell or vengeance in that wrath
            or love transformed by hate's disguise?

Jahweh holds the flaming sword--
            what lies beyond the gate?

        the image of the mirror's front,
        reversed to
        contemplate

Priest or Poet?

They had given me my last meal.

I had asked for Sbarro's pizza deluxe, with extra sausage and extra cheese; I've always loved pizza, and Sbarros, to me, was the best national chain, better than Dominos or Pizza Hut.

It was pretty good.

And I also asked for a large Diet Coke, with ice.

Look, I wasn't on a diet. Most people on death row aren't. But I always drank diet Coke or diet Pepsi, I prefer the taste.

When I was growing up my mother was always on a diet, and she always drank diet cola; and I got used to it; the regular coke tastes too sweet to me.

Yeah it was all pretty good; a good last meal.

But then I started watching the clock. What else could I do? The clock said I had 18 minutes left, before they'd come and take me out to the whole lethal injection bit.

Eighteen minutes and 16 seconds!

Then I heard more footsteps, and the warden came in—

I had always hated his guts. He was a seedy little character with this thin cowboy tie he always wore, a white shirt under his corduroy jacket with rules, Rules....RULES written all over it.

Oh shit, I thought, my last 16 minutes on earth and I have to see this little creep.

"Well,...how ya doin', Mike?"

"How am I doin'? How are you doing? I'm gonna die in about 15 minutes, how about you?"

He smiled.

"That's a nice tie." I said.

"Mike,....two questions,....first of all, if ya have any last words, for the press, ...and you know, all the people you killed, for their relatives,... are you sorry about anything?

"Well,...gimme a couple a minutes,...O.K.?"

"Sure, Mike,......sure......."

"How long do I have?"

"Well, at this time, Mike,....fourteen minutes and twenty three seconds....."

"O.K.,....yeah,...I'm a little sorry,...sure..."

"You are?"

"Yeah,....for that guy in McDonalds,...the guy who wouldn't share his fries with me,....yeah,...I shouldn't have shot him,...him and his baby daughter. I was wrong! But the rest of them? They fuckin' deserved it!"

"O.K.,...Mike,...O.K.   Now,...the second question,...would you rather see a priest or a poet?,...for your last couple minutes,...ya wanna hear the last rites or would you rather just hear some sort of poem?........"

"Priest or poet? You're losin' me, warden. What's the deal?"

"Well,..it's one of these new fandangled laws the atheist lesbians passed through the State Senate,...you can either talk to a priest or a poet,...I don't know,...I don't really understand it much myself,...but it's a new law,....so priest or poet?,......it's up to you. Which do you want?"

"O.K.,...O.K.,....I'm thinkin'......"

Priest or poet? Damn, I only have about 10 minutes left to live and they start asking me crazy questions. I was never very good at making decisions, if something annoyed me I'd just shoot it,....priest or poet,.......priest or poet?.......

"O.K.," I said, "Send in the poet!"

What's the difference?, I only had about 9 minutes left to live, and a priest, I knew, would probably be some queer who would read me a couple of lines he'd stolen from Jesus and then split. The poet would probably be queer, too; but most poets are drunks and drug addicts, and maybe he'd give me a shot of vodka or a line of coke..... ya know,.. so what the hell?.....

"The poet?"...said the warden. "O.K, then. He wants some poetry! Bring in the poetry woman!" He yelled to the guard standing out in the hallway.

A moment passed and the guard returned. He led in a little old lady, her hair was all grey and in a bun, it looked almost like an apple there, just glued on her head.

"O.K.," said the warden. "I'm gonna leave you two alone! This is kind of a private moment, right? But, Mike,....you behave yourself now,...O.K.?"

He left my cell, slammed the locked door. I looked at the tiny old lady.

"Hi Mike! And how are you?" She asked.

"How am I? I'm gonna die in about eight minutes!"

"Now, now,...don't get so negative.....we all have our problems."

Obviously I'd made the wrong decision. This woman was a lunatic. I dashed to the cell door and started banging the bars.

"Warden,...warden! I want the priest!....I changed my mind!"

"Do remember when you were in high school, Mike? You did go to high school, didn't you? Remember Emily,....Emily Dickinson? I'm sure you do. Well, she's my favorite."

I couldn't help but glance up at the clock, I had about seven minutes left.

"Well, I'd like to read her to you now,…I think that you'll enjoy her….."

"No,…NO!"

"Oh, Mike,….let's have an open mind…O.K.?…..Emily was a tremendous poet,….give her a chance….."

"Warden,….I screamed, slamming my fists against the bars, " WARDEN!…I WANT THE PRIEST!"

"So here,…listen, Mike,…."she said, holding a sheet of paper in her hand. She started reading…….

Because I could not stop for Death—
He kindly stopped for me—
The Carriage held but just ourselves--
And Immortality.

" WARDEN!,….WARDEN!----I WANT THE PRIEST!!!"

We slowly drove ---he knew no haste
And I had put away
My labor and my leisure too,
For his Civility-----

"I WANT THE PRIEST!,…WARDEN!" I SCREAMED!

We passed the School, where Children strove
At Recess—in the Ring—
We passed the Fields of Gazing Grain—
We passed the Setting Sun----

(she continues reading the whole poem,…Mike keeps yelling "I want a priest!" banging against the cell bars,…I WANT A PRIEST!")

***********the end**********

86

Goodbye Grandma

while carving the word FUCK
on the tiger's cuspids,
I suddenly spied an intricate
doily lying nearby buried in
the straw not 10 feet away
from my work;

"excuse me a second,"
I told the tiger,
"just keep your mouth open,
I'll be back in a minute."

I hobbled over to it's
symmetry, keeping one eye on
the tiger who so far was
obeying my request.

I picked it up.
what I wondered was this delicate
object doing in a cage?

I was thrown back to memories of
my grandmother,--the polished
wood of her credenza, the smell of
wax and lemon polish.

Through the corner of my eye the
tiger kept his huge oral
cavity open waiting for my return.

My grandmother had a circus
book she used to read to
us at bedtime. I remembered
the smiling faces of the clowns;
the wizened frowns of the magicians --
the terrible wonder of it all

Doilies were in style then, some
30 years ago, they were carefully
lifted during dusting with the
canisters and jars.
Tigers were something we rarely
confronted. The world was a
world of singing birds on
vivid trees in June.

How could I tell her now, if she
were still alive, the terror
I had to resist and master and
how her circus books and love of
doilies became something monstrous
after her demise?

The Marriage Of Homer's Eyes

His eyes were extremely close together. This was one of his major drawbacks. In fact, he would often stand in front of the mirror and pull his eyes apart. Only when he felt depressed. His psychiatrist said it was normal. As long as he didn't try to poke them out.

Today was his day to visit his brother. Homer was on the eighth ward, where he had lived for the past four years. Before that, he was on nine.

As Arthur rode the elevator, he felt his stomach get upset. Why? he asked himself. I've been here many times before, I'm used to it. Besides, every time I see Homer I feel better inside. Somehow.

Homer was sitting in a chair. His legs were coiled up around his hips, that's the way he always sat when he was watching television. He was nearly totally blind. 98%. He was born that way, though not really. It was cataracts, the doctors said. The bad kind. They tried to remove one of them when he was five but Homer woke up on the table, drugged though he was, and the scalpel sliced his eye. That was his first operation. As Arthur walked towards his brother he wondered why he felt so sad. Homer always cheered him up. He liked to hear him talk. It made him feel better.

A young nurse approached Arthur. She wore the traditional white, but topped it off with bright red stockings, which made her look somewhat like a candy cane. Arthur noticed her fat thighs. He also checked out her tits, which bounced like jelly across the floor.

"You're here to visit Homer!" she smiled, "Well now isn't that nice! He does so like a visit. Are you his relative? He has so many friends."
"I'm his brother," Arthur said.
"Arthur didn't like her manner. It seemed too sweet. If there was one thing Arthur couldn't stand it was something too sweet.

"How's he doing?" Arthur said.
"Oh," she answered, "Homer is one of our best. But you should know, I mean being his brother and all. The only time he's any trouble is when it's dinner and we have something he doesn't like."

"Homer," she called, approaching his chair, "Stop your movie for a while. Your brother's here to see you're fine."

Arthur put his hand on Homer's shoulder.

"I didn't know you'd come today, I thought it would be raining."

"No," said Arthur, "it's alright, it's good to see you."

The ward seemed particularly barren today, it always did on Sunday. Many of the patients were out on visits, many were just out for rides. Sunday, of course, was visiting day.

The ward was shaped like an L. The longer half was filled with beds. The two halves met by the nurses' room, which was where they kept the medication. The shorter half was sort of like a play room; television and cards were all they had. A few torn up old magazines, which no one ever read. The retarded patients tore them up.

The nurse retired back to her station. The ward was clear except for Arthur, Homer and an old black man who continually spit on the floor.

"What are you watching?" Arthur asked.

"This is a comedy, I wrote it in fact, if you'd like to know."

"You wrote it!" said Arthur.

"Well that was in my other life, my writing life."

Arthur wasn't surprised, he was used to Homer talking about his "other lives."

"But what about your talking life?" asked Arthur.

"Well yes," said Homer, "I had that too."

Arthur smiled. He liked to hear him talk that way.

It's now time to describe Homer. He was one of the most unusual looking people in existence. It wasn't totally physical. It had something to do with the way he walked. Something to do with the way he talked. He was like the Leaning Tower of Pisa – on stilts. He had a funny kind of drawl, which, though expressive of an unusual intelligence, was also the cause of much humiliation and teasing by the other patients. But he was used to it. It was part of his many "lives."

The metal door slammed, and the food truck entered through the rear.

"Food truck," shouted the colored man. He spit on the floor and then searched his pockets for some tobacco.

Homer tried to stand, but finding himself too shaky, he sat back down.

"I don't like it." he said.

"Oh it isn't bad," said Arthur. "You have to eat, pretend you're in another life."

Homer made the effort. He rose, and Arthur led him by the arm to where his tray was placed.

Arthur was starting to feel better. Homer always made him happy. "Tell me about your writing life," he said, smiling.

"Well," drawled Homer, "you know that I used to be a writer once. But in another life."

"But what did you write?" Arthur was now getting going, starting to feel good. When he felt good he liked to tease.

"Well," said Homer, "I don't know. They say I wrote the Gomer Pyle show."

"The Gomer Pyle Show! Who said that?"

"Well, them! The people. I don't know who!" he shouted.

The nurse emerged, and started to wake the old black man. He was spitting all over his chin. She shaked and shaked. Arthur was watching her breasts vibrate and kept asking Homer, "And what else did you write?"

"Well," said Homer, "I don't know. They didn't tell me."

"Who didn't tell you?"

"I don't know," said Homer, who began to eat his boiled carrots.

Arthur J. Fishmonger. Accountant. Employed by "Barbara's Creations" which was really just a fancy name for a company which manufactured padded bras. Arthur actually had nothing to do with the product itself. He liked it that way. He had no love for padded bras.

Arthur J. Fishmonger. Eight years ago. Second Lieutenant of the 29th division. Commonly known as the "Kangaroos". They all had little emblems made with kangaroos on 'em.

1943. After leaving Paris, they all moved to the foot of France. Most of the people spoke Spanish there, and Arthur J. thought it was romantic. He was only twenty-four. They were on the outskirts of Toulouse by the banks of Garronne River.

"I'll tell you, man," said Tom, "I've had it with these French women. All they want's a lot of money. Now the Spanish are different. They've been through more, and they know what it's like."

Arthur stood in front of the mirror, trying to pull his eyes apart.

"Let's take the jeep," he said, "Hell, you're the second Lieutenant, no one's gonna tell you shit."

Arthur stood before the mirror. He didn't even turn around.

"For what?" he said.

"For what?" shouted Tom. "Fishmonger! Are you an asshole or what? for what! We could take a jeep down to Sebastian, 80 miles away! Fuck some real Spanish cunt, have a couple quarts of beer, and make it back in time for breakfast. Whata ya say?"

"Well, I don't know."

He didn't really like working for "Barbara's." But he had to admit it was a good job. He never worked too hard. He had always been good with figures, and during the army he learned bookkeeping. Six months on the G.I. bill when he came back and that was it. He had never even met Barbara, although he dreamed about her. She didn't need a padded bra, and so what if she did. It's really no one's business.

His eyes were extremely close together. Once in the army a guy had told him that people born that way could never see too much at one time. He never forgot it. He thought about it night and day. Even over his figures. Even in his dreams. In his dreams he sits on the corner of a bed in Sebastian, Spain, and Barbara asks him why his eyes are so close together.

Back at his apartment, the clock seems twice as loud. He enjoyed seeing his brother. But then the nurse came and said she had to cut his nails. They always say that. It's the biggest trick in the world. She wouldn't have been bad though if it wasn't for her thighs. She should do exercises, that's all. Five minutes a day is nothing.

He thought about the nurse. He felt sorry for her. She must've been quite young. When they get old they don't even care. At least she tried to pretend. The old ones don't even pretend.

But what do you do with Homer? You couldn't live with him. You stick him in a dump. You let him have his "lives." You let him throw his baloney at the nurses.

You let him masturbate as people walk by.

He laid on his bed and tried to sleep, not thinking that he could. He didn't take his clothes off. He saw the nurse. She tried to cut his nails. He grabbed her thigh.

"What you need is exercise!" he screamed.

Homer was masturbating in front of the television.

She took off her bra.

"My name is Barbara," she cooed.

He held her bra and began to finger the cups.

"You're not Barbara!"

"My name is Barbara," she cooed.

Homer held the bra in his right hand.

The television fell off the wall. It continued to play.

93

"I wrote this," shouted Homer.

"When?"

"I don't know!"

The worst part of the day is always the morning. That's what Socrates said. Arthur didn't agree. In fact he loved the morning. He loved to see the girls at the office file in. They always dressed so nice. He would sit out on the bench. The bench in front of Barbara's. Sometimes he felt like a sick old man. He could feel their perfume radiating through the air. Even if they weren't wearing any.

All day is was the figures. They kept his mind in place. But he couldn't help daydreaming.

She took off her bra.

Homer started screaming.

"What you need is exercise!" shouted the nurse.

After the morning it was always downhill. He knew he has to call his mother. She'd have to know how Homer was.

"Now, Arthur, is he looking healthy? Is he getting enough to eat?"

"He's looking fine."

All day it was the figures. Padded Bras which bring in dollars. They weren't Arthur's dollars.

At lunch it was Nathan's and the book store. Arthur enjoyed political writing. He dreamed of being President. He didn't really want the job.

He imagined himself at a press conference.

"Mr. President!"

"Yes."

It was Homer asking the questions. He was on Nation-wide television. He asked the President what to do. His eyes were extremely close together.

The President gagged. "I don't know," he said.

The girls in the office filed in. They always looked good after lunch. A spectacular woman walked past, below the sign that said "Creations." Arthur thought maybe it was Barbara, though he couldn't know for sure.

Suddenly they were at lunch together. She was an ex-literature major from Harvard.

"And why do you think Hemingway killed himself?" she asked.

"Maybe he was depressed."

"No, that's not it. He was too intelligent to get depressed," she said. "Your eyes are certainly close together."

Arthur invited her back to his apartment. She had long thin legs and black hair. As soon as they walked in, she immediately sat on the sofa. Arthur sat next to her. Suddenly two drinks appeared on the coffee table.

"I want to be a writer," she said, taking off her bra.

She took off her bra.

Homer started screaming.

She didn't have no tits.

They were all mutilated, and scarred like molten rubber.

"I always wanted to be president," he said.

He was on Nation-wide television. The girls in the office filed in. It was Homer asking the questions. He asked the President what to do.

She took off her panties.

The girls in the office filed in.

They were on Nation-wide television.

He asked the President what to do.

"Fuck me!" she screamed.

His eyes were extremely close together.

Back home. After work, Arthur was having hallucinations. He saw numbers, real numbers, floating around the room. He was sick of accounting. He wanted to be a writer.

At the typewriter, Essay the first. "The Problem of Virtue" by Arthur J. Fishmonger, the writer. He would get it published in the Saturday Review. He made up his mind.

The telephone rang. It was his mother.

"How is Homer?"

"Why don't you ever call your father?

Don't you think he's lonely?"

the problem of virtue.

the problem was he couldn't get beyond the title.

the problem

"Are you still seeing that girl?"

"Barbara, you mean?"

"The pretty one with the long legs!"

the problem

"I don't know who you mean."

"How is work?"

"I want to be a writer."

"The next thing you'll want to be president."

"I do."

"What does Barbara say of this?"

"She's totally behind me."

"Why don't you marry her then, what's the problem?"

"I can't get beyond the title."

Back at work, Monday morning, Arthur felt depressed. He stared at his coffee.

"What's the matter?" asked his assistant.

"Nothing," said Arthur, "Have you ever seen Barbara?"

"No," said Fred.

Arthur picked up the phone and dialed.

"Barbara?"

"Excuse me, please, I have another call on line three."

"Barbara?"

"Yes."

"Barbara, I need to talk."

"Is this Arthur?"

"Yes."

"How are you Arthur?"

"Pretty Good."

"What's the problem?"

"Barbara, I want a divorce."

"Arthur, can we talk later? I have another call on line three."

"Barbara, please, ...this is important."

"Arthur, you've never even seen me. How can you want a divorce?"

"That's why!"

"It will never go through court, you have no grounds."

"I want to be a writer, .. a poet."

"I thought you wanted to be president?"

"I changed my mind."

"Look, I have to go. Incidentally, how is Homer?"

"How is Homer?"

"Yes, didn't you see him yesterday?"

"How do you know?"

"He told me he saw you."

"But Homer's Blind!"

"Are we talking about the same thing? Look, I'll call you back…I have another call. Try to calm down…I'll call back."

"I'm serious, Barbara…I want a divorce."

"We'll talk about it over dinner…try to settle down. I have to go."

Click.

Arthur placed the phone on the receiver. He stood up.

"Where are you going?" asked his assistant.

"I'm going to get a drink."

"But what should I say if Barbara calls?"

"Tell her I'm not here."

The Broken Violin

Emily sat in the dark
at her desk,
looking out her window;
(she certainly thought about death alot!)

Her mind was very hard.

she had trained it to be that way.
as hard as a diamond!

the world she lived in was even
harder--with its labyrinth choices, to be chosen and
formed and cut
by the incisors of her
brain.

she imagined she lived in Texas,
she had never seen an armadillo,
they didn't have any in Amherst

there are armadillo
in texas

April 22, 2000

Hyena machine sucks the mind
of the lame,

        autumnal clouds drip on
        the blindness of Thursday;

not one valid excuse in the bunch.

Sun,...what is sun? Unless you spell it with an O,

Peter and his exterminator group
              contaminate the falling leaves
   and courthouse with no pleasing hymns

Just the hum and hissing of hyena
        (that smart wry prosecutor)
    living off the public dole
       on steaks and caviar

10-26-00

Joining the Human Race

I really didn't want to.....I had tried to put it off
for years--

but after reading the Holy Bible for 19 months under
the influence of heroin, I could no longer see any
alternative,.....

I was certainly stupid and weak enough for the
job,
I was also totally selfish, and a complete
liar,--
not only to myself, but to anyone else
unfortunate enough to cross my path.

I had all the qualifications.....it was true!

but would they accept me?
I was tormented by the question.

And while I felt my own sufferings unbearable,
I found the pain of others
trivial and unjustified.

(another plus on my resume!)

Yes,...I had all the credentials,

    they'd have to accept me,
  I'd fit right in,...

But what if they didn't?--
              I mean, there's too many humans as there is,
        they sure don't need anymore,

        maybe there's no more openings,

(no, that's ridiculous!)
      Oh,
            they'll accept me.
not that I expect them to be nice to me or anything
like that, no....
      they may even take me out back and shoot me,
      or lock me away in a cage somewhere,--
they do that a lot, you know
      yeah,...but I have to take my chances,

I have no choice,--
      I'm
          one of them

January 2001

I WANNA WIN

What happened?
I wanted to be an
artist--a great artist.

I wanted to continue the
work that Christ had
started, change the
world, all that; --

But here I find
myself in a McDonalds
playing their Million Dollar
Monopoly Game--
and
I wanna win.

All I need is piece #53
and I get a $1000 dollar
shopping spree at Sears

      What the hell, --
What would I buy?

What would Christ buy?
or Jackson Pollock?

What would Emily
Dickinson buy on
her shopping spree,

underwear and envelopes?
a black veil?
Does Sears carry black
veils?
probably only through
their catalog service.

What would Hart Crane
purchase?

an erector set and
a deck of tarot cards?
a flower pot for Pocahontas?

Bukowski'd get a power drill
and 4 dozen
pair of stockings to
give out to his broads,

Christ would give it
all away
warning them never
to eat Egg McMuffins
ever again

Verily, Verily

Whitman would buy
$800 worth of first
aid cream and bandages
and a Greyhound

ticket to Gettysburg,
But me, what would I
get with the
$1000?

Ah, I ain't in a
class with any of
those guys,
I've less compassion
and less talent too,
a lot less
I'd probably get a VCR--
and some dresses for my daughters,

I've got as much
guilt as Kafka

What would Poe
buy?

Does Sears carry coffins?

Ginsberg would get a
bunch of mattresses
and lay them
on the railroad tracks
protesting
plutonium

Kerouac'd get
a nap sack & sleeping
bag, & plaid flannel
shirts, all red &
a case of gallow burgundy

Halliday would spend
it all on colored pencils
and crayons.

Corso'd shoot it up,
and if Burroughs won
he'd cut it
up.

They say Hemingway
couldn't get it up,
but if he won he'd
probably hit
the sporting goods dept.

Frost would buy a shovel,
snow boots and a scarf

Pound would buy a ham radio

But what would I
buy?

Damn, a whole
thousand dollars
I could get a new stereo,
yeah and every Madonna
album ever, a Madonna poster--sure,
a CD player, and
Cowboy boots,
a Swiss army knife w/ 86 blades

and a telescope--

a chainsaw, yeah -- I
could start my own business

nah, I'm too lazy--they
would only go to rust
Anyway, I don't think
I'm gonna win,
nope, not a chance,

I just drank 5 cups
of coffee and every time I
get a game piece, it's one
I already have, in triplicate

Well, at least I'm not
drunk--not today anyway

What would
Dylan Thomas buy?
Does Sears sell
stomach pumps?

The Bad Deal Disease
(prelude to a bender)

they tell me it's a
disease, this thing; but to me, it's
always been just
a bad deal.

so I keep on drinking
hoping somehow the deal will
change,
but it doesn't,

cause it's a disease.

THE BAD DEAL DISEASE

and the only successful treatment is
a cactus bush,
and they tell me if I sit on it
long enough,
I'll learn to like the needles sticking
in my ass;

and I'll say,
"yes, I'm grateful I have a disease, and I don't
feel the needles sticking up my ass, I feel them a little,
but I like them, and yes,

God is good and he loves me, that's why he gave me this
disease, I'm grateful he did,..."

but I think they're full of shit.

and meanwhile, lesser men than I drive off in Cadillacs
and sail on yachts, and they can drink martinis when and
if they want to,

but I can't
cause I have a disease;

and the only treatment is to sit
on a cactus bush 24 hours a day
and pray
with a bunch of other idiots--
and it just sounds like
a bad deal to me,

that's it,
I'm sorry.

A most erudite man

After drinking all night
With Edgar Poe,
I decided to take his advice--
I'll never write about talking birds.

3/12/03

trying to figure, when,... exactly when,
did I first go wrong?--thinking mushroom
clouds on a sunny day--yet how in this world
of fallen angels and constant war, can you possibly
go right?--it's all a maze, ...an arcade, a
merry-go-round of lying strangers
selling insurance,... stealing pennies off of
dead men's eyes,....

    this winter I slept in a laundromat, --my forehead
cut & bleeding, my only goal in life being
always to have cigarettes--it's post-historic news,...
dreaming lecherous priests and St. Francis murders,
...the smell of fast food roams the air,...
but if you go east long enough, you'll wind up
in the west, I hope;--
an equation of algebra's misery!
......justice for sale, as usual,
and other verbal diarrhea,
   and a President with the mercy
of a clam;
   I'm watching Sharon Tate on television,
...Valley of the Dolls,... the sound muted;--
Coltrane wailing on the stereo,
...deformity, death and
bad weather hail in another spring;
---where everything growing is also forbidden,
can't remember my own dreams,

   I need to take vitamins,
.....an' hobos with bad feet
      are in trouble

April 2003

HIERONYMUS BOSCH COMES TO LAVALLETTE, N.J.

I dreamed I was Brian Wilson, before he went crazy;

I had just finished Pet Sounds, my masterpiece, and I wanted to send a copy

to the woman I loved, Mary Fitzpatrick (I wrote it for her),

.....but she wouldn't take it, I couldn't reach her,

she liked it that way,....

     she hated me,.........and so I started going crazy....

But what does this have to do with Heironymus Bosch, Lavallette, New Jersey and

the death of democracy?,...well, nothing, asshole,...this is a dream, remember?

........so it doesn't have to make sense, and poetry is a dream, also;

a dead dream,

......murdered by Charles Bukowski fans who drink like pigs and have no need

for innocence and hate Brian Wilson's beautiful music, and the garden of

     earthly delights in his songs,...

    (...think about it....)

  but while I was going crazy pining away over Mary Fitzpatrick and her refusal

to listen to Pet Sounds, I watched a lot of television (to calm myself down),

and I saw Audrey Hepburn in Sabrina (she played the daughter of a chauffer,....and

she was really beautiful,....so I got her address somehow and SENT HER A COPY

OF PET SOUNDS!,....a CD, actually, (of course, CDs didn't exist back then-----

------BUT THIS IS ALL A DREAM-------REMEMBER!!----<u>SO IT'S ALRIGHT!</u>

and Audrey listens to my CD and likes it A LOT!,...AND WE START

TO CORRESPOND!!---

    And eventually she moves to Lavallette, New Jersey, to be

    closer to me (I live in Seaside in this dream),

111

and we start to go to the beach a lot,
(in my dream) and we fall in love (of course),
and even though she is extremely thin
and flat chested,
I overlook her shortcomings
(cause she has the face of
an angel, and I'm crazy, anyway,......)
and the whole dream
works out
wonderfully

logopoeia

when the fog lifts
I say fuck the fog

but when the moon comes
it's impossible

so I borrow one of her snakes
and she tells me of the Parthenon.

the new restaurant
she
means

Antonin Artaud applying for his driver's
License,
brought along Van Gogh's death certificate as
identification,
shouting, "I am not really here! I have lapses into
non-existence!"
                            the clerks were not impressed,
                    using his best Lamont Cranston voice
          he told them he would return
with other documents and maybe some
photographs

                          after leaving the DMV office
he went to a payphone and tried to call Hart Crane
but dialed Edgar Poe's number by mistake
and asked him if he had any laudanum
but would settle for some
laughing gas,
but Poe, (tired of his crank calls)
simply hung up,
after which Artaud bummed a cigarette
off some Mexican, and screamed "I don't need a
driver's license, How can I drive?
....when I don't
really exist!"

          yes, truth takes many
        forms, and life goes
           on,
                although

                sometimes

                        it doesn't

12-6-04

Angels

angels are very popular lately--
television shows, movies,
books about angels,
people selling angel figurines
ceramic trinkets,
one mall I was in even had a cart-stand concession
selling all kinds of
angel stuff;

I don't imagine that real angels
like this very much.

angels don't like being fooled with, I'm sure; making
money off of angels can only bring trouble.

and an angry angel is a terrible thing--
there is very little difference between an angry angel
and a demon.

they come from the same family.
they do bad things when they're angry--
un-angelic things.

you can't test God,
and you shouldn't fool w/ angels
or capitalize on their power
and beauty;

they're closer to God than us,
they're his servants and messengers;

they don't float around
on clouds, smiling and playing harps,
that's all bullshit,

their beauty isn't our beauty,
and their idea of goodness is
not the same as ours,
real angels are scary,
demons and angels are
almost the same,
they explore the same realms
and talk to each other,

and it's none of our business
what they said,

unless they
want us to
know

My father

Father,

as much as I dislike you,

I have to say,
you never conned me,

you laid it
on the line.

the world is a rotten place,
you told me,

our lives are short and
stupid,
then we die.

a lesser man
would have lied.

for that I thank you

Flea Market

The world seems to me
       a very decrepit place
   this morning

     or maybe it is
I who am decrepit
  with 2 hours sleep,
       sitting behind a flea market
   table,

I want to go back to sleep,
      but I can't.

I've things to sell --
   I NEED MONEY.

  I'm not alone in needing money.
          WE ALL NEED MONEY!
   --we're a bunch of
     decrepit people needing money,
(that's one of the things that makes us decrepit)

selling broken cups, and rusty wrenches,
   and Goodhousekeeping magazines (9 years old)
       for 25 cents each,
     and greasy paperbacks falling apart,

and scratched up old Dan Fogelberg albums,
who the hell would want to buy a Dan Fogelberg album?
(his own mother doesn't play his records)
he's the king of the used record boxes;
and there's one dealer,
a nasty old bastard,
sucking on a big cigar (like it was a woman's tit),
standing behind a table with a display
of Lincoln pennies,
with the minature face of JFK next to Lincoln's,
and a poster which explains how --
both were elected in the year 60 (1860 & 1960),
both were assassinated in office,
both had VP's named Johnson,
and blah, blah, blah, etc.,---

and you can buy one of these unique,
collector's item pennies
for only three dollars (while they last)

yeah, ...life is strange,
filled with bizarre coincidences,
---I'll say!
as we hustle and squeeze,
and wheel and deal,
all our decrepit lives,

Cause we ALL NEED MONEY!

and sip our coffees
in the cold
behind our tables,

but at least we're working for ourselves (if you can call this
working),
and we can pack up an' leave
any fuckin' time we want,
and never get fired,
except by ourselves.

and I got a guitar that I'm trying to sell,
an' I think someone's gonna buy it;

people keep asking how much it is, and picking it up and
trying it,
I oughta put a sign on it,---90 bucks!
(but I'll even take 80,...I'm broke)
an' I can't play it anymore, cause my hands gone bad,
Cubital Tunnel---the doctors say,
almost like Carpel Tunnel, but in different fingers,
Carpal screws up the thumb and index,
but Cubital fucks up the pinkie and ring fingers;

they're stiff and numb, and hard to move,
an' sometimes they hurt,

and without your ring finger and your pinkie,
---- you're not playin' any guitar, Jack!
unless you're Django Reinhardt, (and I'm not) ---

he only had three good fingers on his left hand,
yet somehow he played
(and brilliantly, too)

I used to love to play the guitar,
it relaxed me;

Oh, well,...I may as well sell it,...it's not doing me
any good now,

I'm part of a decrepit chain of events,
of destruction and civil wars,...
and Cubital tunnels and two headed pennies,
and crappy scratched up old
Dan Fogelberg records
cause we all need money

and Lincoln fought the war to preserve the Union,....
  and give the Feds the final word,

  and not so much to free the slaves,
    (he wanted to send them back to Africa);
 but the winners write the history books,
and 51,000 killed at Gettysburg in three days!

 one of the reasons the south lost there,
   was cause Lee had a terrible case of diarrhea
all during
  the battle,
 (this is true!)
  back then diarrhea could kill you,
    back in the 19th century;

 and now a hundred and fifty years later
  I'm sitting behind a table at a flea market,
 with my bumhand,
   trying to sell a guitar
  in the cold,
   thinking how much

  I hate Dan Fogelberg

Human Speech Boiled Down

Before the vocabulary of the human race was reduced, people actually spoke to one another; of course, this currently seems impossible to believe, but it's true!

"Good Morning" meant good morning!

"Enjoy!" meant,....enjoy!

"I love you!" ...meant-----I love you.

Archaic concepts, now it seems; for almost anybody with 20% of their brain intact knows full well that no matter the sound or the twist of the phrase, the cadence or the musicality, the tone of words in any various incantation, irrevocably, ultimately, undeniably means, in truth,----

I NEED MONEY!

But how did this happen? How did all words lose their validity and meaning? Before we were afraid to talk. Before the human language was reduced to the equivalent of really only three true words.

This, my friends, is the mystery. And one far beyond my capacity to understand. But once it happened, men and women, being resourceful as well as devious creatures devised several million variants of the phrase - " I need money" to hide their baser, necessary motives.

Whether the sound of the words uttered are produced from the throat of a snake charmer in Delhi, India, or a parish priest in Norfolk, Virginia, the meaning behind the words inevitably boils down into the same, simple, undeniable true meaning, chiefly----

I (OR WE) NEED MONEY!

A newborn baby's first cry of freedom after the initial slap, means essentially,---

I NEED MONEY!

An invitation to any supposedly festive social occasion, be it a wedding, a birthday, or even a funeral inevitably equates into ---

I NEED MONEY!

Obama during his triumphant, historic march to the White House told us dramatically, "Yes we can!"

I joined his website. I liked the guy, I still do. His website told me,-----

I NEED MONEY!

But what is money? And why do we need it? Well, volumes have been written on this subject and I'm certainly not qualified or even able to understand it, honestly. A long time ago, before words lost their meaning it used to be labor and products and barter. But nowadays---it's debt, ...or the absence of debt. I'm as confused as anyone.

40 years ago a guy named Marshal McLuhan claimed the Media is the Message! And we sure have lots of media. And the message surely is,---
WE NEED MONEY!

So, if you have nothing else to do today, and you probably aren't working, since there aren't any jobs anymore, at least not in the United States; maybe you can come up with a new way to say---I NEED MONEY! And if you come up with something new, some new way to say it that's really original,...you might even make some,......

Good Luck, Folks!

Untitled

Life stops
hope stops,
God stops in his tracks of mercy

time and the weather
never stop

streets stop,
music stops,
breath stops,
the finite cry of endings

there would be no time
without motion;

no before,
no after,
a strand of liquid pearls flowing
the string of time's
Illusion

Untitled 2

I don't know too much about
anyone else's personal suffering,
but I do know if your Yin and your Yang
aren't integrated
you're in for some deep shit---

roses and vomit become hard to
distinguish from one another
and gargoyles bake you
birthday cakes,

you find yourself trapped in a huge
shopping mall and there are no exits,
and you haven't a dime---
no way home!

words lose their meanings---
smiles become dangerous and
hellos can be deadly,
and every road
you're on
is the wrong
one

The sorrow of stones

we live between the sorrow of stones,
between the grinding wheels of
ennui and violence;
Pygmalion staring at his frozen love
waiting for a miracle salvation, ...

eros floats through the messenger's lies,
IF ALL IS LOST . . . SOME WONDER MUST BE COMING!

between the axe and the tree,
the frosty dew,
at the expense of innocence ---

>   (the lion's headache has grown so
>   severe, the lion tamer puts down his whip and
>   walks over to comfort him . . .)

we live between the turning pages of non-fiction, . . .
sunrise/ sunsets
waking forgetfulness
kingdoms of absurdities called honorable,
true stories glazed in individual falsehoods
(subjectivity?);
the time of the assassins has reached its climax
projected onto a huge video screen,
the dominos are all loaded
and the jokers totally wild; . . . . .

the broken violin

love falls
from the ceiling lights
around my broken violin,

Billie Holiday picks it up
and walks it over to the window.

"You play this thing?" she asks.

"Yeah," I say "I used to, till it broke.
I threw it against the wall."

"Reminds me of that woman
you loved, but it didn't work out. She
was never yours. What ever happened
to her?"

"I don't know,...I'm not sure......"

"You want some dope?" she asks.
"I got some really good shit!"

"No,...it doesn't help anymore. It doesn't work."

"So you realized."

"Realized what?"

"That you can't own anyone,...you can only love

them." "Yeah,...well,...I don't own anything!"

"Yes, you do!"

"Yeah,..what?"

"You own the broken violin!"

Eight Years
for Eileen

I saw her as a tragic figure,
this bag lady she had become;
but she didn't act so tragic,
she was sort of happy, in fact;
she'd accepted her life
on the street for eight years;
knew dozens of people, hundreds maybe,
was very sociable.
They helped her out sometimes.

She sleeps behind the church rectory
with the permission of the priests,
under the awning, out of the rain.
It's the premium spot in town, better than
the train station, or down by
the river.

We used to be friends and talk;
she claims that one time, when we worked
together for the County, years ago, I took
her to a Patti Smith concert.

I don't remember this.
Sometimes I drink so much
I can't remember weeks, even months;
long stretches of time become
a dim, dark haze,
impossible to recall.

But we don't talk anymore.

One night I was drunk
and I confronted her;
it was out of concern, mostly,
but it didn't come off right.

"Look," I said...."It's been eight years!...you have to
get off the street! Yeah, George was a scumbag, and he threw
you out and took your daughter from you. The first year was
his fault, he was a dirtbag. But the last seven years have been
your fault. It's been eight years! Are you just gonna live on the
streets forever, and blame him and curse him, and do nothing
about it? We've all had bad marriages! Shake the dust off of
your ass and move on!"

"You're a delusional drunk!" she yelled and stormed away.

I apologized a day or two later, but she doesn't forgive me.

I suppose I crossed the line. I do that sometimes when I drink too much.
And who am I to judge anyone? But we all do that, don't we? It's almost
impossible not to.

I like being a hobo sometimes for a while, but after 3 or 4 months, I sorta max
out with it. I start to yearn for a TV, my record collection, a coffee pot,
a place to shelve my books and so I go back to the world of
rent and mean landlords, once again.

But eight years! Damn, and some miserable winters, too;
this woman was beyond
my comprehension.

Wow,...that's anger!

Frank the embezzler

He was probably one of the coolest
guys I ever met, Frank was;

but when the bank he worked for caught him embezzling & his wife
threw him out of his big ranch house in East Brunswick,

he wound up living in this shitty rundown rooming house
in the ghetto on Throop Ave. w/ me & Chuckie
who sold all his food stamps for beer and wine

and it was all downhill for Frank.

He hardly even washed his clothes anymore.

We used to go to AA meetings just for
the coffee, and if no one was looking wrap up a
bunch of oatmeal cookies in a napkin, and stick them in
our back pockets.

I loved Frank, I did;
but back then (in the late 70's) things were looser,
they even gave out Social Security Disability for stuff
like alcoholism,
and when Frank's x-wife in the big, old house
in East Brunswick applied on his behalf,
and he finally received it
he started drinking hard, every day, at least a fifth
of vodka, usually more,

every day,
                until his blood oozed out his
         eyes and his stomach burst open
           like a birthday balloon

a delicate art

Mark walks with hobbling legs
down to the river
with his 12 pack
of Milwaukee ice,

he's tired of living
would rather die.

and when they drove the nails
into Christ wrists,
(it wasn't the palms, it was the wrists)
you can pull the nails out of the palms
and run,

but the Romans were smart,
and everything's science,
and with the nails in the wrists,
no one ever escaped,

they had it all down
to a delicate art!

but Mark isn't Christ,......
there's no covenant here;
no sinlessness,
no sacrifice;

but he'll never escape either.

just a 62 year old drunk
with a bunch of warrants he
can't pay,
tired of living
and getting fines
for open containers

Christmas 2012

Truth--that two edged
sword fell down
somewhere between
George Washington's horse
and Einstein's head
behind Palmer Square.

Reality's like Play Dough, isn't it?
bend it, pull it, shape it into any size,

and Christmas came so fast this year,
some people almost missed it,

pondering dead 6 year olds,
and NRA Romneys hanging
cliffs of cold delirium,
the Maya end
maybe 4 months off;

and -- "it's not that I'm afraid to die, … I just don't
wanna be there when it happens"
(Woody Allen)
everybodys getting older
Mick Jagger looks like Don Knots;

and yet, … there's a place somewhere,
somewhere … far, far away, ….
that's not controlled by the cartoon media,

where Christ really
died,
and we
were
saved

The Sum Total

At the tree

of knowledge

I figured it out.

You can add apples and oranges!

just call the sum total ----FRUIT!

And the serpent was hanging from a branch there,

smiling, saying,.....

"See,...see,....now ya got it, pal!"

yeah, I got it

and the rest is history.

a morbid history for sure.

.....of wars, and pestilence and hunger and death, and

....

.ah, what's the sense of complaining?

yes,

I added apples and oranges.

and the serpent

laughed

all the way

to the bank

English Teacher Small Talk

Ted and I were
in the break room
talking about nouns,
and then we threw in
a couple adverbs;

those conjunctions will
drive you nuts, he said,
not using any adjectives;

I disagreed, conjunctions are
easy, (I thought to myself),
it's prepositions
I can't stand,
they really fuck
with your head!

and interjections can be
a bitch, too, I told him.

Do you have any idea
HOW ALONE AND MISERABLE
MOST PEOPLE ARE!!
he shouted.

What?

You heard me! Diagram that one.

Diagrams?! Diagrams are old hat, I
haven't diagrammed in 20 years, and
I don't expect my students to, either.

You're making a big mistake!

So be it, I said. Everythings mostly verbs
and nouns, the rest is all bullshit. Made
up by old ladies, who haven't gotten laid
in ten years,....

You think that if you like, but you'll never
get tenure with that kind
of attitude.

Maybe you're right. But then I'll just take
my verbs and nouns
and go somewhere
else

9/4/14

computers and the law

no one's free anymore
computers know everything you do,
nowhere to run.

idiot laws hold us
helter skelter like veins
that pin us down,
circulating from state to state.

no more getting the hell out of Dodge,
Dodge follows you;

no more shaking the dust off your pants
and starting over
in another town,
it's all one BIG TOWN.

Big Brother's BIG TOWN!

(yeah, but Orwell had one part wrong),
Big Brother's more subtle,
more insidious,

he calls himself Sweet Jane,
we play him on our smart phones,
then download another song,
and snap our fingers to the beat,

and the beat says--
"you can't run,
it's over."

and the next song we're gonna play is --

War is Peace

(I love that tune)
It's got a good beat
and you can dance to it

I give it a 95!

Le gusta este jardin?
Que es Suyo?

looked up the cheapest place to live in
the U.S. over the internet,
but somebody else found the refrigerator box
before me,
then my laptop froze up
(it does that a lot).

I'm not unique.
I just wanted to be another Dylan clone,
mopping up Graceland's floors,
another lilly in the field
shouting some poetic waste,
but things just got out of control!

had to go back to the beginning, back through
the whole fuckin' thing, --
how Cephas became Peter,
and his three denials,....all that...
had to study it.

But the Pentecost was the best part!

And someday I know that miracles will be
so commonplace, we won't even call them
miracles anymore (maybe that's happened already)

There is hope.

and William Blake and I will go
out for lunch, and I'll pick
up the tab,....and "Bill," ...I'll say,..."Billy,.....

get some onion rings,....you love onion rings!"

and Christ that thorny Tiger will
sweep all the courtrooms
of everybody.....
everybody but the Judges!
and boy, are they gonna sweat!
we're gonna need another Noah to mop
up all their tears,....

yes,

but for now,....right now,....I'm just gonna get
another cup of coffee, and
finish reading Seven Story Mountain,
and hope,

Evite Que Sus Hijos Lo Destruyan!

Was He Ever Really Alive?

there are more and more deaths nowadays,
there are more and more people;
and after I hear someone died, sometimes I have
to ask myself,...
was he ever really alive?

Did he ever really love another person more than he loved himself?
Did he ever sleep in the rain, in a graveyard, thinking, "this makes
perfect sense....."
Did he ever take a chance so slim, it's like walking on a razor blade with
an ice cube and it's 120 degrees out, and lose (of course) and then do
it all over again just for kicks?

Did he ever curse the robots of this world
and try to buy a hot gun in the ghetto at 1 a.m. in the morning?

Did he ever ponder Christ's words and start to cry, and want to kiss his
hands and kiss his feet?

Did he ever throw everything he had away, thinking,..."So as
the birds are clothed?...."

Did he ever wish he could take a time machine back to 1936 and want to
shoot and kill that fucking Hitler and save 6 million innocent lives?

Was he ever really alive?

Did he ever realize black people are just as smart as white people (if not
smarter) and certainly a hell of a lot tougher!

Was he ever really alive?
Did he realize we're born into this world to love and suffer, and they go
together and are intertwined, and if you don't do either you were never
alive;
Was he ever really alive?

Who Loves the Little Fish?

the big fish eats the little fish
powered by legality,
a power false but driven by the
pardon of the world.
the world it grows upon
crab claws, as decades
roll and yawn,
amoebas climb the surface scrolls that
line our yellowed walls;
the Spirit, though, it still believes in truth,
(the Rising Tide!),
and loves the little fish the most,
who swam and rode,
and died

12/13/2015

Marble Comp: Journal Poems & Fragments from Note Books

CHRIST that beautiful animal
        jumped through a wheel of FIRE
    leaping whale's oblivion
    eternity

        houdini-ized that sick diamond
    tree
        behind a cloud,

Jack-Flashed Rose
    w/ a gallon of port
                and then some....
(hell, i didn't even hear the crash,
when the lightning struck his flowered
armor................i was in my prison
cell,...   memorizing old dramas, and
                                worst)

CHRIST THAT FEARLESS CHILD
ran wild cat in the mortuary

        emitting stars, and new songs
endless,
        his ladies lovely knees
    another weeping
                        angel

in the temple again

circa 1990

Business is the Serpent

business is the Serpent,...yes,...
usura-----hey!.....
the tail between the tigers legs,
the blunted ache of morning stone;
our bread, our bread…
as if the air unscrolled a curl upon our
heads --

a curl of snakes!

yet men and women must survive,...
but how in a world of houses and food?

"the bread, the bread," our babies cry,...
We love their curls, yet hate their
cries;

the snake, the snake,
our fears devise,
oh,...business is the serpent's guise

September 1991

I Stand In Doorways

between rehearsals I
sometimes cry,
and stand at doorways
doomed to enter;

and ride the sea a
thousand miles,
only to die and
be reborn

potential corpses shake
my hands,
I cannot hear their
footsteps fall,

the crash of waves
it drowns the sounds

I never really
heard
at
all

the philanthropist always becomes
the philistine –
all beautiful, wholesome apples
ground to rotten, decaying pulp;
hyenas cackle in the
alleys—
the snake is on the run.

monks pour wine down
yapping mouths,
the sun climbs the
mountain unsung, doomed
by the turning
of worms that devour
the dumb

9/2/92

Mandalas chained to the
hexagram rain, w/ a candle
that drips on the floor;
Forbidden Fruit, the grey
cloud spawned,
machines clicked down
a hill –
Achilles yawned,
the day had dawned, and
Coltrane blasted
a furious trill

9/3/92

these hands, eyes, mouths,
in a burst of thunder
    Freedom viewed –
        Freedom! – that dream
    agent – known mostly to
    convicts and children –
    too terrible to actually bare,
    or put to task;
    the hands, eyes, mouths,
    ran back into their T.V. caves,
    content to polish prison
    bars, and wash old martyrs'
    feet of clay

9/4/92

the dog the child loved is gone,
so is the post the dog was chained to.
so is the child.

gone, all gone;
the yard not the same yard,
the house not the same house,
the people, the people,
gone all gone.

so time is a huge stone; and also the
absence of the stone—
on which nothing
I knew remains…

9/7/92

the incongruous flood of the hydra laws
ruined the fisherman's holiday,
and left all the whales on the beaches
without so much as
a word to say!

in keeping with Octopus' dreams of clay
and bloodbaths that washed all their
plans away

past elections were all ruled invalid,
and the dictator sharks
given mastery

9/12/92

refuse, refuse, --
the taxidermic light from
the window
the pimps disguised as
Uncle Sam,
the skull and crossbones
veiled as God,

refuse, refuse,
and then walk into another
room

9/13/92

breeze stroked the cheeks
of the citizen worm,
leaning on trees of desires
that burn,
dogs yank their chains
and bark at the maze
that falls in the core
of our grieving;

Every face in the line
shows the trace of some
crime, it conceived and had
thought of committing and the
slow pull of time
that mercy cast down
settles like dew
on the evening

9/14/92

conflict creates energy
in the celestial pantheon,
and on Main St. too.
Conflict tears the worm
with the beak,
conflict cements the lover's feet,

"conflict creates energy,"
growls the tiger gnawing
a bone,
conflict sends the armies
home

9/15/92

Into perpetual harmony
swings the earth's pendulum frames,
innocence rests on it's axis
of logic,
but it's mountain's pour
lava and flame

9/16/92

The scapegoat hated many
people, he wanted to undo
them, so he acted coy,
and took their blame.

The man who invented the
key of G understood this.

Poe stood in the mortuary,
pen in hand, and looked
at the animals. After one
died, he called it his lover.

The man who invented the key
of G understood this, too.

The wind is like a heavy bear,
it growls and destroys, but
more often than not, is
asleep and calm.

The man who invented the
key of G knew this well.

What he didn't know well
was how to make money
and how to get along
with his wife.

9/17/92

Sleep is kind -- we forget the
rain -- the fractured
armadillo under the porch.
we forget the stone people,
their cruelty and lack of faith
-- the jigsaw puzzles of our
minds -- the
days tedium.

The chess pieces were in
the wrong place the entire
time-- the clock was broken,
a cricket sang outside the
window "When the Saints
come marching in".....

Elvis was truly dead and
the Colonel was selling
his eyebrows

9/18/92

150

The tarantula had legs that
danced over God's spine,
over and over. There isn't
much difference between a
parachute and an A-Bomb
until the last second.
Death itself, like a parasol
is sometimes feminine; when
viewed from certain windows
and pain has the softness of beautiful
cobwebs and stained glass.

9/19/92

it's not enough just to be
alive,
you have to waltz w/
the dragon,
you have to stare into
the inferno till your eyelashes
singe, then withdraw just
in time;
you have to be able to
say you've been there,
really been there, and
came back again
better for it

9/23/92

no care at all for vipers' fangs
or drowsy emperor's thrones,
the length of journeys magpies sang
so distant from their homes,

the leaves of quick refusal heaved
the breath of summer's rain,
Jaguars sped to mongoose caves
to lick away their pain,

the baboon's head was thick with sleep,
it's eyes of lead were glazed and deep,
a snake slid round a cactus tree
and pointed to Eve's misery,

the power of money not yet known,
nor civilization's chewed-off bones,
two lovers bodies tied the knot
and sealed the blame the dove forgot.

9/25/92

industry pulses through
the can man's veins --
no fool, this old man,
canning pays!
he stalks the streets and
parks like a gazelle

9/26/92

Flea would walk and walk and walk.
Where? Nowhere. Anywhere.
And think and think and think.
Bout what? Nothing. Everything!
And pray and pray and pray.
For what? To whom?
He wasn't sure.
He simply wasn't sure,...ah,....to God!
What God? (there's more than one)
He prayed to Flea's God, the god of fleas.
The god of fleas that walked with him on his journeys
to nowhere/anywhere,....the god of fleas that understood and heard
his many, many endless flea thoughts as his consciousness circled
round and round in his flea brain.
And Flea hoped his flea god heard, he sure did. As he walked and
walked and walked and
thought and thought and
thought his endless flea thoughts and
prayed and prayed and prayed his endless
flea prayers to his own personal flea god,
he sure hoped he heard.

9/27/92

Flea was starting to
believe that the "crime
commits the criminal."
Pretty subversive stuff.
His girlfriend, Polly,
told him he was starting
to lose it, you know…
going nuts. But Flea
was unperturbed.
"See," he told Captain
Lockjaw, "that only
proves my point,
the crime commits the criminal."
But Lockjaw was losing his
patience with Flea. "Flea,
take your chicken or
egg shit and stick it where
the sun don't shine."

9/29/92

Money -- what is it?
the drug of security, the
badge of honor, responsibility?
real value's untouchable.
real value can't be destroyed.
but what of the greenbacks
we hold in our hands?
words like love and God have
been misused, twisted and destroyed
by power, the power of money.
the dim, stain hiss of
civilization; a civilization
more brutal, more deadly than
a viper's sting --
power destroys the meaning
of words, the value of
money

10/3/92

crawling through the dirt
searching for a place to stay
and food to eat, Art
takes its proper perspective:
that of a luxury.
   But alas, why we're alive
isn't something to be sneezed
away, either. Trees grow
from vast craters of emptiness,
valleys rise and fall in the
eye of the mind's direction;
what is and what isn't aren't
so easily divined, hammers
of rain pound down on the
soul's huge complexities and
to survive just isn't enough;
the imagination needs to
roam freely and devise
morality plays…

10/5/92

delicate porpoise dichotomies
   trace the wear on an old Roman coin,
   Medusa's head yawns and flies over
   the map of a coast she destroyed;

a bomb is sewn into the carpet of a hall
   where an Emperor kneels,
   breaking the backs of his children
   whose torture is always concealed.

   10/6/92

In this digital world
everything you say is true:
objectivity died w/
the steamboat --
     up in smoke!
I'll trade you my blind spot
for yours, said the
good lizard to the good
snake as the atomic
rainbow melted the walls,
I'll sell you my horns
for 80 fine blind spots,
the latest currency,
cheaper than gold --
the arts and crafts of
Armageddon

December 1996

Hope / Doubt

sometimes I think
that maybe Jesus isn't
still alive, maybe he
didn't rise from the dead,
get resurrected;

maybe he was just a
cool guy, the greatest
poet and The Sermon
on the Mount was like
his Woodstock,

but even when I have
doubts, I still think
he was a great man,
who gave mankind hope,

hope even over death,
a chance of seeing
our loved ones again,
a chance at redemption

3/29/00

I AM THE WEATHER

I am the weather (no,
not a weatherman, they're
all pretty faced assholes
from Vassar)

I AM THE WEATHER!
mean, and kind,
hot and cold;
   I'll drive you blind,
w/ ways so wild….
you'll run back home and
   cry for mama…

  I am the weather!!!
the soother and destroyer,
  like Shiva w/ a
    horn from hell, or
    Christ-like w/ my gentle sun;
      that pops the flowers from
      the ground, and
    wheat and corn to
      feed your kids

I suck the wind out of
your lungs and beat you
till you're sore,
  the soil it turns upon
  my whims,

I am the weather--w/ a
devil's laugh the size of
China,

and weeping farms
upon my knees,

I am the weather.....drunks
they like my cold/warm
flush upon their withered
cheeks

I am the weather!!!
--the biggest size of
everything.....washing
out baseball games
just for spite...
and you just bought
a ticket.....fool!

I am the weather--
w/ a Juno whore on every
arm...
I suck the flood's cunt of ancient
rains and turn them
into famines leaping...

I am the weather!
--so take your myths
and spin them on a
crooked pole,
I am the weather!
scorn of hookers.....and cops!
House painters and
mailmen;

I am the weather
and my only boss

is stuck inside the winding stars,....

I am the weather!.....
so you'd better build your
houses strong,....

cause I'm comin'
through w/ claws

May-June 2002   162

the poison of money
drifted up on the beach,
Skee-ball and five dollar slices
of pizza,
a horseshoe crab w/ the
mark of an angel;
terrified luck -- it comes
when it may,
in the eyes of blind dice
and hooker pleasures,
911 used to be
an emergency phone call,
things change,
artists die, change their
styles,
climb fences
to new dimensions

3/15/03

Carousel

it's voodoo;
the frozen boardwalk
glistening in 10 degree wind;
a dead bird told me spring
is coming,
but not today
a dead man walked out of
an elevator without any
shoes, he pulled out
a gun,
a huge clown face
it's paint peeling off
grins at the ocean
thinking of flight

3/29/03

it's not important --
the sound of waves
crashing on pier posts,
neither that
nor the late coming of spring,
nor the bicycle cops
riding the boardwalk;

the old God's are what's
important,
the dead Gods,
the ones who plundered
and raped each other
to death

they echo in the thunder clouds
omens and
rain and
broken umbrellas

4/12/03

I don't feel bad today,
I can't hear the bombs,
I'm deaf in one ear,

and the stars last night,
the stars shone like they do,
like as if
there were hope,
and I'm deaf in one ear,
and the bombs if
they're falling,
are far, far away

when the winter is gone,
and the sea warms the earth,
it is almost as if
something's starting somewhere

and the cold and the greyness
and winds move along,
and I can't hear the bombing
it's miles, miles away

4/28/03

the sun drips for a
huge cavity of
souls,
its white hot flame
upon the carnival's
darkness within,
illuminated
destruction on our
concrete mercies,

aware of this
I only pick up
pennies if they're
heads down,
tails up,
no matter how
badly I might
need one

8/2/03

Grasping at straws
in a continuing stream of bullshit
I decided to apply for a
job decorating ice cream cakes
down the street

The sign said "no experience
necessary – will train."

What did I have to lose?

I really needed a job.

I had a minor degree in
art from Trenton State College
when it was still called
Trenton State College.

I could tell them that!

Only one problem – I'm a 54 year old
drunk and drug addict – and I
need a haircut – I'm starting to
look sort of like Charles Manson.

My NA sponsor said I should
apply anyway

2005

The idiot and the moron

The idiot told the moron
To blow it out his nose,
But the tide was high,
And the moron sly,
So he blew it out his toes

Then the idiot in anger
Grabbed a huge iron mallet,
And smashed the wicked moron
In a place that never heals;

It's a story without virtue,
And a common hand to play,
For when idiots meet morons
The stakes are high all day.

Pluto (1930-2006)

August 24th, 2006
Pluto is declared
an un-planet; (or non-planet)
They've taken its planet-ship away.
Fucking shit!
God-damn fucking humanity!
First they make you a planet -
give you a little dignity,
a little prestige,
then they take it away,
bunch a creeps, aren't they?

How do you feel
                today, Pluto?
How do you feel?

Like a non-entity?
Like a piece of shit?
Like a fucking worthless
piece of rock
floating in outer space.
Like a fuckin moon?
Reduced to being a
big fuckin moon?
Moons are shit.
No one cares about moons
                any more,
lover's don't even sing
        for moons - not
            anymore -
        They're old hat!
        Stupid cliches.

Planets are something!
You were a planet, once.
One of nine!
(Albeit - The smallest and & furthest away) -
But you were there - The 9th Planet!
                    Now what?
Do you feel like
Marlon Brando in On
                    The Waterfront?

Well, Pluto I sympathize
            (or is it empathize?)
Anyway,
I thought I was
important once,
a long while back,
I thought I was
a poet - I was gonna
be a poet, a great
poet!
But no,
The poetry police
told me otherwise.

Who are these people?
The poetry police?
And the planet police?

They're the same assholes
that name street signs,
that's who.

The controllers,
The power people -
            assholes all of em.
The people who tell
            you you spelled a
            word wrong

Well, I didn't spell it
        wrong -
            you spelled it wrong.
            I spell it the way it's supposed to be -
The way it should be,
in a fair world,
in a right world,

a world where Pluto is
The ninth planet
& where I'm 23 years
old and a great poet
            and lover,

Fuck them, Pluto,
you'll always be a
planet to me.
Always!
Pluto, the ninth Planet.
Discovered in 1930.

God Bless you, Pluto!

2006

POLICE RECORD

I'm proud of my
Police record
I don't want it expunged!
It's the police record
of a good person
who just used to
drink too much.
It's good to drink too
much when you're
young,
but I'm not young anymore.
I'm proud of my
Police record
I want to keep it
forever
and I never really
did anything bad
even when I was
a drunk
Why should I get it
expunged?
Why?
So I can get a
Good job?
There are no good jobs,
probably,
Anyway how can it
be a good job
if you have to
pretend you're someone
you're not?
I like my police record

and I never really
did anything wrong,
just lots of stupid shit,
sure,
when you're young you
act stupid.

But I'm not young anymore,
and I'm not stupid either
my police record
is the proud
history of a
stupid drunk who
was young
and thought life
was fair,
but found out it
wasn't, & tried to be
free
and that's
O.K.

12/5/08

the moon eclipses over
the dead.
We like to hide
the dead
like we like to hide
our money
our dead money.

I've circled round
the sun for 64 years

haven't learned a
goddamn thing;

cept love is better
than pity,
though sometimes
they
intertwine

9/27/2015

MY DEAR FLIBBERTY GIBBET

the worm in the ball
has eaten the core

and the dark sun...
carries a cloud away

God Bless the Child
that's got his own
in F sharp
w/ claws
diamonds on the thru-way,
and falling moons
in garbage lots

Editor's Note

I published Matt's first book <u>UPTOWN DOWN!</u> in 1999. It contained
38 poems, all of which are included in the first section of this book.
All of the poems in the *Uptown Down!* section of this book were
written in the 1980s and 90s.

The Marriage of Homer's Eyes was written in the 1970s when Matt was an English
and Art Major at Trenton State College (now The College of New Jersey). The story
was published in the college's literary magazine *The Lion's Eye*, and won an award.

The poems in *The Broken Violin* section were written between the years 2000 and
2015.

The poems and fragments in *Marble Comp*, the final section of this book, were
transcribed from Matt's journals, which he kept in Marble Composition notebooks.
They are presented here as journal poems and fragments, not as completed poems.

Other Iniquity Press/Vendetta Books by Matt Borkowski

<u>UPTOWN DOWN!</u>, 1999; out of print.

<u>The Reincarnation of Shelley & Other Poems</u>, 2017.

<u>SCORPION</u> (aka *PLASMA DONOR*), 2017.

Made in the USA
Middletown, DE
05 December 2017